Growing Grace

Stories from the Herb of Grace

Gardens, Nursery, Shop & Tearoom

Bobbie Cyphers

ParterreWilde

Bobbie Cyphers

i

ParterreWilde

parterrewilde@outlook.com

ISBN: 978-0-578-98291-5

Cover Photo by John Cyphers

Printed in the United States of America

To Kim

My child, my heart, my remembered joy

Author's Note:

This is a book of memories, all true, subject only to the vagaries of memory and of time passing. With this in mind, I have changed the names of most individuals and obscured the setting of more than a few places in order to protect the sacred privacy of both.

So to those of you – miracles all - who shared our journey, "Thank You."

And to Molly Wilson, editor most remarkable, I am eternally grateful.

Illustrations

© iStock.com

Table of Contents

Growing Grace

This used to be among my prayers – a piece of land not so very large, which would contain a garden, and near the house a spring of ever-flowing water, and beyond these a bit of wood.

~Horace, Satires. 35B.C

Before...

We followed the sun westward away from the city. Trading vegan bistros for mom and pop cafés, we soon passed into the littered margins of liquor stores, pawnshops and tanning salons. As if shaking free of all the detritus accumulated by a weary humanity, the road swerved right and commerce ceded to suburb. A few miles on as the horizon swelled, small brick houses on low hills gave way to silos, hay bales, white-faced cows and mailboxes propped up by barbed wire fences. At ever-lengthening intervals, roads of dirt and gravel sprouted along the highway to crawl north or dip south around tobacco barns and through cattle gaps, disappearing into the mystery of hollows and coves. We had not traveled this way before.

Narrowing, the highway began to swoop and climb, taking us along for the ride, and like a river slicing ever deeper into the earth, it had carved out banks head-high and rising. The landscape swept past, dappled in sunlight beneath stands of poplar and oak older than any surviving generation of man, finally surrendering to Stygian darkness under hemlock and pine. Time seemed to inhale, breathing in the present then flowing back into the past. Slowing. Without warning, the road veered right, skirting sheer rock face slick with moss and lichen; then just as abruptly swung back, and we were looking down on where we'd just been. Over the next six miles, through dense forest, along vertical ridges, whiplash always threatening, the road would switch back upon itself twenty-three times.

About the third mile, or it could have been the fourth, or even the first, we passed a tiny house – abandoned, but straight and true and tidy as if the creatures of the woodland kept watch, took care.

"It was right there," visitors told us later, as they watched the little house disappear behind them, that they just knew they were lost and would be left to wander until they became old bones.

But for those of us who did not turn back, who kept going, who crested the next ridge, the forest briefly fell away, and the world sprang free, released to a sky that looked fathoms wide and eternally high. At our backs lay the city of Asheville. Ahead, layer upon layer of forested mountains rose and fell. The silvered mists of the Blue Ridge shimmered around us.

"Ah, there be magic," we said.

Down was another direction altogether, and we slipped again between tall poplars, the road twisting and dropping, drawing to its side and in its wake the icy waters of a mountain spring, bubbling from beneath the earth. Joined by other springs, a trickle bred a torrent, and the waters of Clear Creek – liquid crystal born out of the rock and stone and mountain – somersaulted, dove, gushed toward what waited below. And road and river, together, descended past old cabins little more than a jumble of pick-up sticks, past ridges haunted by old dreams. Through light a billion years old.

At the time, beautiful as it was, it seemed an ordinary bit of wonder to us, starting over in a valley carved out of the mountains by time eternal. But that first day, we had no idea where the road would eventually take us. What grace awaited us at the beginning of every day. And what grace would be bestowed upon us at its end.

And shortly thereafter...

A slightly worn and weary pair of travelers climbed over that mountain, having learned over time to set the bar of expectations about Limbo height. Nevertheless, we found a small farm clinging to a south-facing ridge in a valley hidden deep in the heart of old mountains – a place filled and stirred with eccentrics and seekers, friends and neighbors, teeming with critters, both prescient and magical under every tree and every bush; and alive with the eternal, breathing miracle of the green and burgeoning earth. We signed our names on a number of dotted lines and unpacked our belongings into a

15

little white house beside a creek fed by living waters. And then, contrary to the clamoring of naysayers and common sense, I decided to start a business and a life. Salvation supplied courtesy of one jewel of a daughter, Kim, with an eloquent touch for getting the news of my foolish dream out into the world and a saint of a husband, John, with the good sense to keep his day job.

Location? The middle of nowhere. The timing? Blessed luck and providential coincidence dumped me in the path of a fast-tracking storm – the early 1990s, and GARDENING was becoming the fastest growing, most enthusiastically embraced pastime of all times.

But all the same, my mother and my grandmother and her mother before her would have said I'd also landed myself in the middle of a hard row to hoe and a very short string to be starting with, but, oh my, did we have fun.

Here then is a book of tales, gleaned from days and days of memories grown at The Herb of Grace – Nursery, Shop, Gardens, and Tearoom. Memories as sweet as wild mountain honey and as potent as blackberry wine.

Act One

In the Beginning

The kindest word to describe the little white house, perched on its little green hump, was "utilitarian." Harvested from stands of dying chestnuts, its beams and sills and rafters bore the mark of eternity covered over with 1940s concrete siding. The house first squatted three miles up the road. Then, the story goes, on a particularly steamy day in the summer of 1950, somebody swatted a fly, rocked back, looked around, and said to another somebody, "Let's move."

And with that they found a neighbor with a bulldozer, help with felling a few standing poplars, and a crew to hoist the house on top of the resulting logs. A few long days later, the house came to rest on its new block foundation – still shuddering from its three-mile downhill roll. Before the first snowflakes fell that winter, father and son added a wing and a porch, and their family of six moved into the five-room, thousand square foot house.

It was now on offer to us, and I was not impressed.

While the house might go unnoticed in an empty field, the barn owned its adjacent hill – a grandfather of a barn, a character of an edifice. Much older than the house it, too, was built from chestnut, before the blight of the early 1900s moved over the mountains like a malignant cloud, leaving in its wake standing corpses of once magnificent trees. Some of the boards were two feet wide, straight, true, and heartbreakingly beautiful.

Dug into the hillside, the lower floor comprised a tractor bay, a central stall with feeders, and three separate storage rooms. We poked our heads in the door and inhaled the scent of decades – alfalfa and clover with a base note of sweet cow's breath.

Upstairs, massive doors pocked with lichen and age slid back on iron wheels, screeching along tracks to reveal a cathedral rendered in wood. We stood awestruck, watching sunlight filter through vertical breaks like lancet windows in the chestnut boards. A chapel smelling of feed sacks and burley tobacco. We looked up at the beams – nave high and a foot thick.

Then John looked over at the 1950, 8-N tractor. Famous in a past life as a cultivator of high-grade marijuana, it had been thrown in the real estate mix by the sellers. Impressed or not, with that my fate was sealed.

A breeze greeted us as we stepped out of the barn, playful, as if it, too, colluded on the sale. Below the barn, the land flattened. At one time, before burdock homesteaded and Johnson grass welded it together, it might have been a garden space or a tobacco field – running to three, four acres. Turning east, we looked across a drainage ditch – the realtor's "lovely little stream" – to another patch of level ground, broken only by the hump where the house sat overlooking a rectangular depression, origin of said hump. From the measurable center of this ill-conceived bowl of packed clay, a silver maple stood alone in a sea of grass shorn to a buzz-cut. On a rise west of the house, another former tobacco field circled a Blue Spruce, achingly lovely in its desert of khaki green. Pointed out with pride by the seller, a single line of sulfur yellow marigolds stood at attention along the driveway; the only other sign of life an unidentified rhododendron, parched to a leaf curling bronze, drooping in its sunny patch next to the cellar steps.

That was our beginning, a rather pedestrian plot upon which to build an unrealized dream. Well, except for that barn and that creek across the road, and the hawk banking against the sky.

Our welcome to the neighborhood showed up on moving day, nosing her way between the truck and the mailbox, speculating her way past boxed books and household goods, fondling our roadshow antiques and vintage finds, collected and transported many a mile over many a year. Dressed in a man's plaid shirt tucked into the elastic waistband of her jeans for matronly figures, Millie handed me a plastic gallon jug, sweaty with condensation.

"I made 40 gallons of cider off that Stayman Winesap up your hill. Folks lived here before just let'm lay. So I come one day and told 'em that was wasteful, loaded up the apples and took 'em with me"

Millie introduced us to most of the people along the creek, up the coves and hollows, with a defining comment for each. The man who owned the cider press was "A hippie, smart as all get out. Went to college – marine biologist. Now he lives with his chickens."

And the couple who owned the café at the crossroads, "Retired with money. Took that old house, duded it all up. Self-appointed mayor of the community. Did a lot of good, though, for the kids when they first come."

And what defined her, she shared in that first conversation, sitting at the bottom of the porch steps in one of a pair of old wingback chairs.

"My only child, Gregg, MIA Vietnam. Twenty-eight years," and she jiggled the bracelet given to the mothers of missing soldiers.

No pain could be worse than losing a child unless it is not knowing if he's hungry, if he's cold, if he's tortured, if he's alive. As one mother to another, I embraced her, holding on for want of words.

20

Her next sentence informed us of the likelihood we'd be blown off our feet by the hellacious winds roaring through this wind tunnel we'd bought. One breath along, she started listing the ingredients for her coconut cake. Said, "Write it down!"

There was a time, she told us, when a general store occupied a corner every couple of miles along the two creeks running through our valley. Selling chicken feed, hay, patented medicine, cans of beans and Spam, flour, sugar, and coffee, they did a brisk business after harvest. If someone didn't grow or construct a needed commodity, they could trade for it with a farmer just up the road. Overseen by a principal, teachers and every neighbor within sight, their children attended a stone schoolhouse over by Big Creek. Factor in the doctor practicing along the lower banks and the one operating above the creek and a person never need leave the valley. Unless they wanted to.

Enough did after the wars to silence the mountains, believing as they did in the promises of a better life in the cities. Only those who could not bear to leave the call of the whippoorwills or the smell of heat rising off the meadows stayed, preferring to have their fellow man some distance removed.

And then, as Millie told us, in the '80s and '90s the tide swung to flow in a southerly direction. The hippies, the disenfranchised, the disillusioned began to leave the cities, to "come back to the land." The fine old country houses, fallen on hard times, were resurrected and dream catchers hung in their windows. Here in our valley, these folks built a volunteer

21

fire department. That self-appointed mayor and his wife, Herb and Em, helped reopen the school, sold nuts and bolts and rented movies at their general store and, alongside, served up fresh rainbow trout, fresh vegetables, and Tuscany inspired pasta dishes at their Creek Café.

The first week after our move, we ate at the Creek every night, passing on our journey the tiny wooden chapel they built in gratitude.

At the end of our second week, in one of those encounters orchestrated by the fates, we met our first friends by way of a crowded Friday night catfish fry down at the café. Weak at the knees from the smell of hot hushpuppies, John and I surveyed the room to an accompanying 120- decibel roar. From across the room and three tables down, we spotted an arm waving us over. Only later, after meeting mammoth-hearted Lenny, did we figure he had to be standing on a chair. By the time we wormed our way over, six smiling faces and a half-dozen heaping helpings of fish and fries welcomed us.

Millie caught us up a few days later, or tried to, "I see you met with that bunch from up the ridge and over in the holler." But by then, we and the bunch – Lenny and Babs, Buck and Sally, Jack and Liz – felt at home in each other's lives, and I steered her out the door and into the yard.

The truth, Millie had everyone in the valley pretty well pegged – adding a little tart sauce to make of us all a better story. Two weeks into our new adventure, she'd equipped us with abbreviated, albeit opinionated, biographies of most of our valley neighbors.

But outside our new old house, an empty canvas trembled in anticipation. I could stand to wait no longer.

In the Garden

Abraham Darby and Friends

It began with a rose. Before I unpacked pots and pans, before I stored the sheets in the cupboard, before I hung clothes in the closet, I opened a box of books and rescued a catalog, an elegant English rose gracing the cover. Enchanting photographs and enticing descriptions blossomed from its pages – new offerings to America from David Austin and his Shropshire nursery where breeding old souls into new roses had been his abiding passion. And now possession, obsession, was within my grasp.

Between cleaning paintbrushes and shaking out curtains, I pored over Damask-scented 'Gertrude Jekyll' and the perfection of blush pink 'Heritage.' Passing over golden 'Graham Thomas,' I instead coveted the apricot elegance of 'Sweet Juliet.' I couldn't decide. I wanted them all.

Sunlight slanted through the kitchen windows as I slotted the last spice from the last box into the cupboard next to the stove. I needed fresh air. I needed to be outside. Grabbing the rose catalog, I walked out into the barren grassland that surrounded the house, lapping up against the barn, spreading to the road. The sun warm upon my shoulders, I drifted across the grass, escaped around the corner, and startled a woodpecker, mining for bugs above the back bedroom window.

I sat down, back to the wall, and opened the catalog to the first page and looked at the picture – 'Abraham Darby'. "Tall shrub – short climber. Strong fruity fragrance. Shades of apricot. Disease resistant. Repeat bloomer. Named for the English Quaker who played an important role in the industrial revolution." I made a call.

While Abraham journeyed from an East Texas nursery to a small farm in Western North Carolina, I began preparing the ground to make him feel at home. I dug the hole – with pickaxe and pry bar. The soil, though rich and black and voluptuous, frosted the sides of boulders the size of Mini Coopers. When I managed to lever enough rocks from the twice-as-big as the root ball hole, the remaining dirt feathered into the cavity, forming a little knoll the size of a morning's coffee grounds. I peered over the sides. A bead of sweat slid down my temple and dripped off my chin, reinforcing the coffee metaphor.

Across the road, the creek cascaded, swirling, churning up black gold. Behind me, up in the woods, another kind of black gold hid beneath a layer of decomposing autumn leaves, nutrient-rich compost for the taking. I dumped a bucket of it into the hole, stirred it together with the little knoll. Hopefully, Abraham would be happy and well-fed.

Arriving bare-root, Mr. Darby appeared bony but sturdy, whispering his promises. I left him to soak his roots in a 5-

gallon bucket of water while I dug most of the soil back out of the hole, leaving just enough to fashion a small hillock in the bottom. Straddling him over it, I steadied his bottom and began to sift dirt over roots. Tamping down the soil, I gave it an extra pat and, as my finale, built him a moat and filled it with fresh spring water. Sitting back on my heels, I surveyed the resulting three-foot square planted plot in its sea of grass. It looked hopeful.

Autumn passed. Winter lingered. Spring broke. Gentle rains fell. Flushing with rising sap, Abraham leafed out, set buds. They swelled. And as if kissed by morning, petals swirled open in a confection of an apricot sunrise, growing ever paler as the light trailed outward from the bloom and its heart. Like Dreamsicles – the color, it looked like Dreamsicles, ambrosia of the past, melting over your hand, dropping down your shirt, landing on your Keds as you race from Gainey's store home, getting in one last lick. And the fragrance – like sitting in a bath of rose petals eating the peaches and cream of childhood.

In one season 'Abraham Darby' reached the window; the next, it had climbed to the top of the window, arching over, giving the woodpecker excellent purchase as he hammered away, checking for grubs.

With that one rose, the little house looked loved at last. So I planted another one, an older rose this time. Introduced in 1930, 'New Dawn' arrived at a time in our country's history when hope was a fragile thing. I can imagine the breeder who witnessed its first bloom – in color and form a new dawn.

Leaning over, inhaling its fragrance, he would have tasted tea and honey. Never have I seen a rose more conscious of its grace and elegance as it draped the arbor John built over the front walk, dangling its blushing blooms to enchant all who passed through.

For the herb garden I planned at the entrance to an old grape arbor, I reached back to the time before the War of the Roses and planted *Rosa gallica officinalis*, the Apothecary rose, the red rose of Lancaster.

Another afternoon early in the year, tired out from painting the porch, I slumped to the ground against the south side of the house. Huddled in my barn jacket, I held a copy of Botanica's Roses. Coming to bask along with me in the pale sunlight, Pet our marmalade cat, climbed onto my lap. Protected from the wind, we could feel the wall releasing its heat stored there by the sun. Opening the book, I was soon lost in the romance of old roses.

On a sultry day near Charleston, South Carolina, in the early part of the 18th century, a Frenchman, Philippe Noisette, gave a rose to a rice planter, John Champney. This gift, the China rose, given the name 'Old Blush', grown for upwards of 500 years, or more, was crossed by Champney with the 16th century *Rosa moschata* in the early 19th century, creating a new classification in the world of roses, the Noisette. One of the most honored of its progeny 'Mme. Alfred Carriere' now grows behind the gates of many a Charleston garden.

I looked up at the blue sky, felt the warmth from the wall, above me the window that would one day open out from my tiny shop to the garden below. 'Mme. Alfred Carriere', with her lush, cupped, flesh-stained white blossoms smelling of pomegranate and peaches and lemons would grow tall against this sheltered wall, her blooms nodding upon the windowsill.

Another of David Austin's English roses joined us that first year. Three of them, actually. The 'Cottage Rose,' soft pink, fat cabbage blooms on small, rounded bushes, peeked out between newly divided irises on a hillside terrace – the aroma of grape soda and old rose mingling in the soft summer breeze.

Out, Out Damned Junipers

There were bad days in the beginning when all I could see was our hard work swallowed up in a dog patch of grass and weeds. Mornings when a hummingbird found an open door and an invitation turned into a death. Evenings when Abraham's first blooms went unnoticed while I wrung my hands over the paucity of my plantings. And what did it matter that 'Mme. Alfred Carriere' glowed like the angels in the morning light when a rabble of ruffians, masquerading as *Juniperus horizontalis*, were muscling in on her territory, making her shudder, pulling her skirt of glorious green aside? The junipers had to go.

We'd need a bigger chain. That's what John said as he surveyed the gnarled mass of trunks and needles. "Yep. Heavy duty."

Out at the barn, he rummaged through boxes until he found the mother of all chains – inherited through generations of farmers back to the folks who'd cut the timber to build the barn. Maybe dropped by them into that wooden box in anticipation for a resurrection to do a good day's work.

John backed the Ford F-250 into the driveway, hooked the chain to the struts, the other end around the first juniper and eased forward. Gave it a little more gas. There was a slight disturbance, a few needles fluttered as if thumbing a nose at us. He lowered his foot on the pedal another notch. The wheels began to spin. The juniper looked mean, hunkered down, didn't budge. John took his foot off the gas and let it idle. He waved me over.

"Damn," he said.

"What now?" I asked. Waited.

"Back up," he said. I stepped off the driveway.

"More!" I scurried another few feet, looked at his face, scurried another ten or so.

John backed the truck up until its bumper menaced the juniper. Holding the brake pedal to the floor, he revved the engine, released the brake and spun forward, popping that juniper out of the ground like a well-toasted muffin. Landed roots up in the back of the pick-up. The procedure was repeated twice more. The remaining junipers surrendered without a fight.

For days I walked past the gaping holes. Stepping between them, I'd peer underneath the porch, then turn to admire the brickwork pillars – beautiful in their simplicity. I relished all that emptiness.

"It looks a little like a bomb site," John said.

Springing from each depression, juniper roots looked not so much snapped off as chewed by ravenous beasts. Ants snaked across, intent on colonizing the hummocks beneath the dandelions, already making themselves at home. I looked down amongst those weeds, and as if the destruction had cleared the path to new beginnings, an idea stirred, dropped a seed, and, at last, The Herb of Grace took root and began to grow.

Bearing Fruit

Apples from the old 'Stayman Winesap' lay scattered everywhere — in the chicken run, down the sides of the spring-fed stream, and rolling like lively children down the hill into the garden. Duffy, our Golden, gave chase with each new fall, dizzy at the bounty raining from the heavens just for him. Retrieving first this one then that one, he laid them at the feet of his lucky humans, his triumph evident in the perforated grin of his teeth marks in the rosy offerings. And still more clung to the branches, rouged crispness waiting to be picked. The sky burned an eye-widening sapphire, the air saturated with the tang of carnival ripeness. And it was long past time to do something with all that abundance.

Carrying one bucket for the harvest and one for the rejects, I made a start among the runaways slipping across the garden path. After a while, the firm, blemish-free apples grew scarce, the spurned looking more and more like little severed heads. After imagining the first wizened crone, I couldn't get her out of my head, desiccation wrought by decay looking pretty much the same in *Malus domestica* as in Homo sapien. I looked, again, into the bucket. A lot of ancestors there. I gathered as many as I could carry in my apron and headed inside to the kitchen.

By the time I heard Millie's morning knock, the apple heads were lined up on the worktable. "Baking a rotten apple pie?"

I sighed. "I thought, maybe, apple-head dolls?"

Still chuckling at her pithiness, Millie circled the table, prodding one old gent, poking another old lady-in-waiting. She told me of Ella "over in Lonesome," who used to make dolls, offered to call her for me.

Conducting her customary survey of the kitchen, she picked up a bowl I'd filled with autumn leaves, squinted at it, set it down, straightened a stack of cookbooks. "I came to tell you that Ben over on the Patch has his cider press up and running. Shame you're letting all those saps go to waste like that. They always did make the best cider."

From the first of Millie's knocks on a reluctant door, we'd heard about Ben. "A PhD'd marine biologist." He'd washed up on the creek some years back and made himself at home, become a friend to all. He turned his hand to a lot of enterprises, fruit pressing being one of his fall undertakings.

When we arrived with our truck-bed load of apples, cider making was revving up to a fever pitch, fueled by the belch of exhaust from an old John Deere. Aficionados in overalls swarmed around Ben's pulp-pressing apparatus, a melding of art and science. In his usual state of Zen-like suspended animation — somewhere between Cheech and the taxi-driving Jim Ignatowski — he sat at the helm, guiding apples into a stainless steel hopper. A giant screw attached to another steel plate, looking like an early experiment by the Marquis de Sade — if he shopped at the local salvage yard — descended. Apples became pulp. Then through a series of ever-decreasing mesh screens, clarified juice was siphoned off through a spigot and pulp became cider.

Every now and then, Ben levered himself from his seat, stopped the press and emptied the filtering screens of the macerated skins and mash onto a fermenting pile. During one such maneuver, a couple - new to the creek - sprinted forward with buckets to scoop up the succulent pig fodder. Ben raised a hand, lifted one finger. Chastened, the woman removed herself and her bucket to the sidelines. Humbled, her companion filled his and retreated. A good-looking Rhode Island Red took his place, pecking around the edges of the pulp pile. At his squawk, the rest of the poultry family joined him. Under siege, one hen with an especially tasty morsel took off at a fluttering run, clearing the cider press and flying straight for the front door to Ben's cabin, just ahead of the remaining flock. I looked over at Ben. He didn't raise an eyebrow.

Over the years the old apple tree rewarded us with a decent harvest every other year. We often wondered how the tree continued to live, gutted by age, all hollowed out by time as it was. Fruit as well seemed too much to ask of the old Stayman, a gift we didn't deserve. But we never again had the glut of apples of that first year, our cider reduced to just a couple of gallons to share with guests on the Verandah.

Drunken Pomme Tart

Night before

> Soak slices from two 'Stayman Winesap' apples in a cup and a half of cider for a couple of hours.
> (Hard cider if you have it.)
> Drain.
> Preheat oven to 425 degrees

Crust:

> One stick butter
> 1/4 teaspoon vanilla extract
> 1/3 cup sugar
> One cup all purpose flour
> Cream butter, vanilla and sugar together. Add flour. Process until dough forms a ball.
> Place in a prepared spring-form pan and press dough over the bottom and up the sides an inch.

Filling:

> One-8 ounce package cream cheese
> 1/4 cup sugar
> 1/2 teaspoon vanilla extract
> One fresh farm egg

In a food processor or mixer, blend cream cheese, sugar, and flavoring together. Add egg and continue to blend until smooth. Pour filling over crust.

Topping:

Place drained apple slices in concentric circles over the top of the tart. Sprinkle with sugar.

Place pan on a baking sheet and bake for ten minutes at 425 degrees. Lower temperature to 375 degrees and continue baking for 25 minutes. Ovens differ, so keep an eye on it after the first fifteen minutes.

Enjoy!

The apple-head dolls? With the best of intentions, I'd dipped them in preservative and rolled them into a half-bushel basket until I could get around to studying the manner of construction. After a while, Kim suggested I add a guillotine and a tiny French flag waving over the basket. Instead, she painted a sign that read "DIY Apple-head Dolls." A few weeks later I passed the basket and noticed the heads had shriveled to resemble "dearly departed" apple-heads and were beginning to smell a bit off. I fed them to a flock of disinterested chickens. Millie said I just didn't get the seasoning right.

Historical Note:

Even Millie hesitated to hazard a guess as to the Stayman's age. "Older than me. By a long shot."

We do know a Malus domestica called 'Sops in Wine' was introduced into the UK in 1832 as a good cider apple. With a sizeable leap, we might judge it a possibility that the American 'Winesap' – origin unknown – might be a descendent. Also known is that a Dr. J. Stayman, renowned hybridizer, in 1868, noticed a 'Winesap' seedling in a promising dozen planted in a Leavenworth Kansas field as being exceptional. Selected and named by and for Dr. Stayman, it proved to be a vigorous grower, producing fruit for the first time in the early autumn of 1875. By 1890 it was one of the most popular cider apples of its day.

And up there on chicken hill, its offspring – looking like a home fit for a country troll – made its debut on the creek long before our Miss Millie made hers

In the Nursery

The Soul of Grace

If the gardens contained the soul of The Herb of Grace, the nursery held its heart. In the beginning, there were herbs, just a few - lavender, rosemary, thyme, parsley, sage - bought in as liners (rooted cuttings) from a wholesale nursery in Michigan. I found their ad on the last page in the spring edition of The Herb Companion. Stumbling my way into the ways and means of the nursery industry, I began to find closer, larger liner providers, but I never found a better one. When we found a new variety or a patented plant we wanted to try, wholesale liner nurseries proved invaluable.

Our first potting bench, an old pine table left over from a former barn in a previous life, occupied a corner of the barn, our first potting shed. And there I was happiest. Like a child at a magic show, I watched torn stems turn into roses, a piece transformed into a whole - the alchemy by which I might participate in the resurrection of a 'Yolande d'Aragon', a Perpetual Damask, whose ancestor graced the gardens of Anjou, or a poppy growing from a seed dropped on Flanders Field.

Delivered as a kit, our first greenhouse - anchored, erected, screwed together downhill from the old 'Stayman

Winesap' – was a Gothic dollhouse. From these beginnings we grew, adding hoop houses and potting sheds, perennials and vines. And roses.

Behold the Rose

Old Roses, I love their stories. Intrigue, loss, abandonment, romance, jealousy, love – green, twining tendrils running through our human history.

She was the first antique I coveted, the first I possessed. Living through more than five hundred years of history – the Renaissance, the Black Death – she spent the French Revolution hiding, crouched at the base of a walled garden just outside Paris. The storming of the Bastille took place mere meters from her home. Called by her acolytes 'Cuisse de Nymphe Emue', she escaped across the channel to Victorian England, her progeny taking the name 'Maiden's Blush,' aware of their adopted country's sensitivities. Keeping her new name, she sailed in the bowels of a tea clipper to a new country, made landfall in Charleston Harbor. And there I was, hunched over my muddy feet in my former South Carolina garden enraptured by the translucence of her shell pink petals, enchanted by the primal memory of her fragrance. From her, I took a cutting and another generation of the 'Maiden's Blush' rose rooted and grew, beginning another chapter of her story in my sister's garden. 'Dolly Parton' may be a rip-roaring stunner of a hybrid tea, but her family tree is still working on its first branch.

In the days before the internet, I devoured garden magazines, nursery industry trade publications, state nursery association member lists, following plant trails wherever they led me on a scavenger hunt for old roses. I found them waiting on a hillside in Northern California tended by a soft-spoken woman passionate about the roses *gallica*, damask, *alba*, and bourbon – a heraldic romance of Renaissance roses. A few days after my call, her catalog arrived in the mail – two sheets 8 ½ by 11, front and back, descriptions like poetry. It took days to pare down my list from the eighty she offered to the twenty I thought I might afford.

While I waited for their arrival, I walked our small farm looking for an appropriate home for our court of old roses – 'Duc De Guiche' and 'Hippolyte', 'Mme. Plantier' and 'Ispahan', 'Rose de Rescht', 'Tour de Malakoff', 'Mme. Hardy', 'Tuscany Superb', the achingly lovely 'Leda' and dating from the War of the Roses, *Rosa gallica officinalis*, the Apothecary rose. Time running out, I settled for a flat, former tobacco patch in front of the barn – the side which bore the kings of the Orient and their star depicted in lights, lit for Christmas, year after year.

When they arrived, the package soggy from its trip, I lined them up in two rows of 10. The last to be settled in new ground was the Apothecary, the oldest cultivated rose in Europe. Settling to my knees, I looked out over my little kingdom, knowing tomorrow I would take the first commercial cuttings from those old beauties.

The nursery grew, and suddenly, it felt like looking after 10,000 toddlers, all clamoring for a drink or a snack, all at a different time. I was now taking cuttings from the descendants of my old roses, left to grow on next to the barn, unheeded, forgotten.

One early May morning, rain drizzling outside, found me in the potting shed, bumping up lavender cuttings. Grabbing the fingers of my right glove between my teeth, I yanked it off, then my left. Five trays down, six to go, and at the end, my hands would be saturated with the fragrant oils of the lavender. Who minded crusted fingernails when your fingers smelled like Provence?

I worked in silence - teasing apart young tender roots, fluffing new barked potting soil over them, settling them gently into their new homes. Moving the trays to the back of the shed to water them in, I glanced out the door. The drizzle had stopped; the sky clearing. Out toward the barn, a shaft of sunlight pierced the clouds, striking an impression of crimson velvet caught in a snarl of head-high weeds. I grabbed my gloves and the sickle hanging by the door.

Led as much by my nose as my eyes, I hacked away at Johnson grass, burdock, bindweed to release a neglected rose, a confection of rubies and fragrance. Bending down, I pulled the tag from the detritus of seasons of falling leaf litter - 'Tuscany Superb.' Further down the row, I rescued another old *R. gallica,* 'Duc de Guiche.' Its blowsy magenta blooms,

47

washed in violet, smelled of old rose and nutmeg, and next to it, an *R. alba*, 'Duc de Cambridge', petals swirling in hues of rose, purple, and pearl.

Groaning, I tore the last of the weeds from the end of the row and stood. Behind me, twenty old roses breathed in the air of the coming day. Freed from the thick, humid jungle of weeds with little sunshine and even less air flow – those roses stood unblemished, not one trace of powdery mildew or black spot marred their lush green leaves – not just surviving, but thriving.

They Called the Wind Victorious

We erected our first greenhouse - the tiny, Gothic, Plexiglas one - on a run of unusually calm days. A year later, when we'd outgrown that one, the windowsills, two hastily assembled cold frames and a piece of plastic stretched over PVC, we bought our first commercial hoop house - small and used, a starter - from a perennial grower who'd keeled over one day, leaving the business in the hands of his son, who lost little time posting an ad in the paper and selling lock, stock, and hoop houses to the first arrivals at the nursery gates.

A hoop house, shaped like a Quonset hut, is basically heavy milled plastic stretched over a metal pipe frame. Someone - we - digs the holes to set the posts, then assembles the bones. As a final step, one checks the weather report.

We'd set the frame and run the wooden nailers in October. Long days of sunshine. Perfection. And then it was November. One Sunday, we looked up from the breakfast table realizing neither one of us had anything pressing to do that day, so we set aside a couple of hours to stretch and staple the polymer skin over the 10x24 foot frame. No rush. We poured another cup of coffee, shook out the pages of the Sunday paper. An especially incendiary editorial required our attention.

Dishes done, we stepped out the back door, stepped back in to add sweatshirts, and then paused to grab a jacket. The temperature had dropped a good twenty degrees during our linger around the table. Silence greeted us. The dogs had buried themselves in the barn. The chickens still hovered on the roost. Far overhead, black clouds thundered from peak to peak. We failed to read the signs.

A preternatural calm enveloped us as we spread the plastic out the 24-foot length of the hoop house, anchoring it with a boot apiece. We each grabbed a corner and raised our hands above our heads, like rustled cowpokes fearing the worst. At that precise moment, almost as if it had been scripted, the wind roared over the mountain, charging straight for us; the only thing tethering us to the ground was that extra layer of clothing. The plastic billowed, heaved. A final buckle and the wind tore it from our grasps, sailing it like the Black Pearl over a sea of grass and potted plants, over the barn, up the hill.

At the top of the ridge, a row of poplars held fast, plastic pooling around their trunks as a hush descended upon our valley. The heavy milling proved its worth as we drug the covering back down the mountain over briars and snags and anchored it with boulders off our wall. Battered, we stood to try again.

We finished by flashlight. That was when we added a step, about checking the weather.

The next year we added two new hoop houses from the manufacturer – twins 15-feet wide and 70-feet long. We had checked the weather report and the next week was to be mild and uneventful. Just a little kite-flying breeze. Early October, we offered a little extra cash to a couple of neighbors to help assemble the metal bones. Time to layer the skin. Thinking of last year, we asked Kim for a little daughterly help. After further thought, we gave Ruby a shout. Neither tipped the scales at much over a hundred and ten pounds, but with nice weather, it would be a matter of light ballast only, maybe a little dexterity.

Taking off both Monday and Tuesday, John laid out the schedule – stretching the six-mil over the heated house one day, the cool frame the next. All necessary tools had been staged; pull ropes lashed to the grommets, awaiting the eight a.m. whistle.

Over coffee, we listened to the weather radio. Light wind, partly cloudy, high of sixty degrees. At 7:50, we stepped out the door, checking the sky. A few cirrus clouds danced overhead. A playful breeze tousled my hair. We headed over to the gravel pads.

Stooping, knees bent, John and Kim grabbed the end ropes while Ruby and I positioned ourselves at the remaining two. Ready. Hand over hand, the plastic slipped smoothly over the curved pipes. Just as the skin reached the apex, Aeolus, Zephyr, Vayu, Njord, and possibly even the old Slavic god Stribog ripped through our little valley, pirouetted and then cursed us from the other direction. The plastic ended up on top of our neighbors' barn, half a mile away.

We wrote another step. Solicit help of ten very large, very strong Vikings.

Through Winter Snows Arrives the Sun

For days the sun brooded, hiding behind dark-bellied clouds threatening snow. Opening our doors for spring in less than two weeks, I kept assuring myself that we lived in North Carolina, after all, not North Dakota. There would be an end to the gloom.

By myself in the greenhouse, reasonably warm from the toasting propane heaters, I wore layers of flannel and wool as backup. I'd finished checking for adequate moisture, aphids, white fly. Everything looked okay – huddled and miserable, but okay. Like me, awaiting the sun. Chores done, elbows resting on stacked bags of potting soil, I daydreamed, lost somewhere on a tropical horizon.

And then I heard a beautiful sound, a UPS truck gearing down. It turned in the drive, and I landed back in the here and now. Ripping open the box with my handy box cutter, I peeled away the tape, scattering aside rice hulls, wading in a pool of fragrance, basking in my sweetly delivered sunshine. Looking up at me, the season's new lavender and scented geranium varieties trembled with excitement.

Savoring my solitude moments before, I now felt an overwhelming need to share. I called Duffy into the greenhouse. He dutifully nosed the box. Lifting laughing eyes, he gave me a Retriever smile, then curled up next to a brooding bunch of Clematis cuttings, sighed and drifted off into doggy dreams.

Alone, but not alone. Me and my lavenders – 'Fred Boutin' and 'Sharon Roberts' and 'Pastor's Pride' and... From the very bottom of the box, I released 'Sleeping Beauty', who would go on to become matriarch to generations of her long-stemmed, delicate, purple progeny. 'Silver Frost' who even in infancy stood apart with leaves glowing ghostly in the garden at twilight.

Underneath a scramble of spilled potting soil, bits of green and slithering hulls, I found a packing slip, note attached.

"I'm sorry I won't be able to ship the remainder of your order. My husband was helping in the greenhouse and sprayed cleaning solution by mistake. I'm not sure when, or if, I'll be able to fill the order, so am attaching a check for the difference."

Sandwiched between the south wall of the hoop house and a solo row of tender lemon verbenas, a parterre of potted lavenders and rosemaries awaited their seasonal debut on the sale tables – cuttings taken from unpatented varieties delivered from this same nursery two winters ago. A single person enterprise, like me, she had welcomed another ally into this grand horticultural life. Like me, she probably waited out the poverty season with a lot of prayer and crossed fingers resting on a stack of unpaid invoices. I felt guilty for cashing the check, but relieved. I knew, even as I faxed the order last fall, I had no business indulging myself to such an extent with her long list of herbal delights.

In The Shop

A Sign to Find the Way

I'd designed that sign in my sleep, as I drove, as I gardened. After all, it was meant to convey not just a business but also a sense of place and a life of meaning. I wanted it to represent a thousand dreams of a thousand souls I hoped would pass this way in the first week or so. It needed to look like it cost a fortune, but fall within my humble budget, appear elegant, yet simple. Class on the cheap. Rather a hard balance to strike.

On the way to the supermarket, to the post office, or on a trip to visit family, I noticed signs. I started out looking at other storefronts, then churches. On my way to see Kim, I saw one in the distance – lovely colors. Swinging from a pole in front of a blue block building, it proclaimed, "Get your Buds, Suds, and Studs." Not quite.

I finally found what I envisioned hanging outside the door of a dentist's office in Waynesville, thirty miles south over Betsy's Gap. Circling the block for the second time, lost, on my way to give a talk on heaths and heathers to a local garden

59

club, I spotted it. I pulled into the parking lot, climbed out. Two birds, one stone, I'd ask directions while trying to explain the importance of a sign. Inside, the front office smelled of cloves, the pervasive fragrance of fear and pain. Instead of an aggravation, the receptionist seemed delighted at my question, finding it refreshing after the patients' usual queries, she said. She held up a finger and punched numbers into the phone. The dentist's husband had been in charge of the sign. I left with a number and directions.

Their mouths full of lemon cake and nuts, the garden club members looked at the clock and managed to nod as I walked in the door.

Weeks later, outside the sign shop, as I climbed out of the car, a bluebird sang. As I walked to the entrance, strains of "My, oh my what a wonderful day" floated in on a warm breeze. The sun smiled. Inside, my sign ready and waiting, beamed. A three-foot by two-foot wooden oval, sandblasted to form the words "The Herb of Grace" in graceful Gothic font, tastefully rendered in dove gray with Oxford blue lettering and trim, encompassed all my dreams.

Even before a sugar pink, vanilla-scented *Clematis* 'Mayleen' climbed the post and draped gracefully over the sign, covering the words, cars blew by – oblivious. Taking the curve at a fast clip, the drivers showed no sign of slowing down, just shoved it into overdrive, hitting the straight-away doing sixty, my lovely sign rocking in their wake.

Then I read the article. The one that listed the minimum size and best color for signage in front of retail establishments, even going so far as breaking it down to cars traveling by at forty, then fifty, then sixty miles an hour. By their calculations, a person cycling in a leisurely manner on a Sunday afternoon would have to stop, employ the kickstand and spend several seconds to make out the Gothic lettering on my beautiful and tasteful little sign.

In a small isolated mountain community, your neighbors notice everything – clothes left hanging on the line over night, the rump of a raccoon upended in the trashcan, the weekly mow neglected. The sign hung for five days, demurely soliciting customers, soliciting comments, soliciting door-to-door salesmen. Nothing. Down at the café for Friday night pasta, no one mentioned it – the elegant script, the decorous color choices.

At one point that first year, I joked about hiring dancing girls to perform underneath the sign, of maybe renting one of those neon ones, flashing – Open! Open! Open! I never did, but years later, after someone stole my first little sign, I replaced it with a bigger and brighter one, and then another carved in stucco and lighted – both still quite tastefully done. We do still wonder how we missed the guy on the bicycle, pedaling toward Trust, our sign clutched under one arm. Or that's how the neighbors described him, later, down at the café.

Are you Open?

Days passed, my lovely little sign swinging on its hinges as every vehicle blew by on its way to somewhere else, failing to attract a single soul. Day ten of my less than successful opening dawned. By noon, I had swept the porch for the third time, tweaked the displays – this basket for that one, the rosemary in front of the watering can – and hung my head in a "My God, what was I thinking" brown funk when a car pulled into our three-car parking lot, carved from the original driveway and a ditch bank in close proximity. In a mood of glass-empty negativity, I looked for a copy of the 'Watch Tower' in her extended hand.

Instead, "Hi. I saw your sign."

In fact, she'd seen it a total of six times. Three trips down the mountain for a home health visit. Three times back. She just couldn't tell what it read until she pulled to the side of the road.

"Actually, I saw the plants. Then the sign."

Memories are so often starred or tainted by what comes after, making me question whether she truly smiled with understanding or laughed in delight, but I am sure she, my very first customer never questioned my sanity in hanging my shingle where raccoons outnumbered people three to one. After our greeting, she picked up one of the baskets I'd been shuffling and started to fill it, first in, a lavender, 'Provence', then a rosemary, 'Jean Davis', and a thyme, lemon. With a sigh, she sank to her knees, ruffling the head of a gray *Santolina*, and chose the middle trug from a graduated display of three. She opened the door to my shop and sighed. Weak-kneed with happiness and relief, I stepped behind my make-shift counter.

Both basket and trug sagged with treasures as she left, turning back just before passing beneath the arbor, still anticipating its rosy future. "I've always dreamed of quitting my job and doing something like this myself. Finding this place is almost as good." She smiled. "Almost."

Necessity spent that first dollar, but hope, rekindled, framed the receipt.

To Market, To Market

A wonderful piece of luck came my way, even before we made the final move to the North Carolina farm. Ten miles from our home, bordering Table Rock State Park, was the little town of Pickens, snuggling up to the mountains of upstate South Carolina. Two blocks off Main Street in a tiny brick building, "The Butterfly" emporium provided us with used books, small antiques, and collections of all sorts. Its owner Mary Jean, a gracious Southern woman of immeasurable generosity and enthusiasm, greeted everyone as the dearest of friends come to visit. One noon, standing at the counter with my $3.00 worth of books – P.D. James and Ruth Rendell – I got up the nerve to ask her how she started her business. I spent an entertaining hour listening to her story. Among her pearls of invaluable advice – start slow, part-time; buy what you like; and for heaven's sake carry jewelry (it was many years before I heeded this last bit of advice) – was an invitation to be her guest at the upcoming March show at Atlanta's AmericasMart, three high-rise towers devoted to the goddess of consumerism. Mary Jean's charge – two nights on the sleeper sofa in Kim's apartment.

Atlanta is not for the faint-hearted. Downtown Atlanta calls for the soul of a gladiator. That my child braved these streets, this traffic, every day manufactured nightmares. Mary Jean and I, both country bumpkins, arrived at the market on Williams Street white-knuckled. Arriving to the morning sun reflecting off acres of glass, tons of concrete and steel, bridges flying like buttresses to connect the Merchandise Mart to the Apparel Mart, finally spinning to the 21-floor Gift Mart, I figured we needed a map and another page of directions. The next two days blurred into colors, smells, textures as we navigated through a bazaar of tantalizing wares. We never moved beyond the first seven floors of the Gift Mart.

I seldom bought at the Market, except for a sweater, once, at a buy-now vendor when I realized my chenille shirt was unraveling to reveal my bra. For one thing, I couldn't take the pressure of instant retail decisions totting up to hundreds, even thousands, of dollars. I made contacts. Some like European Soaps I still buy from today. The Market is where I learned the ropes, of minimums (how much money you have to spend before they let you buy), lead times (how much time you have to give them in order to receive your merchandise on time), and, most importantly, the trends. One of those trends entered the Market the year after I opened my doors. "The Gardens" occupied an entire floor of the Gift Mart – expanding the second and third years to take in part of the floor above. Gardening was hot.

Once we opened, John and I traveled together every year in January to Atlanta. We seldom had time to move beyond the Temporaries – new artists, new businesses – and The Gardens. We fell in love with obelisks, arbors, gates, and all objet de fer, saw at first hand the meaning of treillage. Arbors with gothic arches, trellises with fleur-de-lis, benches, tables, baskets. So much of it to wade through. And the pots. Glazed in translucent French blues and reds and greens, or aged to a patina worthy to grace a Tuscan piazza. Surrounded by wind chimes, birdhouses, garden aprons and clogs, I almost wept with delight.

The first year, we discovered two brothers who replicated historic architectural remnants and a manufacturer of pots that would have pleased Josephine and her citrus trees at Malmaison. We took home brochures, business cards, catalogs and ideas and dreams. It took a few years before we were able to meet the brothers' minimum and ordered a Celtic cross, spitting and sitting gargoyles, shelves on the backs of cherubim from the brothers. We never did manage the $2500.00 minimum order from the pottery manufacturer. But a small Southern entrepreneur from Birmingham sold us an array of her antique reproductions. One, a three-foot-tall urn, faded sage green like the original Florentine antique, never made it to the shop, dwelling instead in the garden, surrounded by lavender.

In the Garden

Eye of Frog and Spittle of Snake

Debbie was the first to knock at the garden gate – our first employee, for want of a more accurate description. Platinum hair like Dolly Parton, khaki shorts tight enough to etch her thong lines, skin still young enough to shrug off her drinker's nose.

"Hey. I need a job."

And here I was on my knees in a bed of nettles, desperate. Full-flowered spring and no help in sight. Until now. "Do you know how to weed?"

"I helped my Papaw with his tobacco." As evidence, she extended her hands, fashion nails an inch long, striped pink and black. Then flipped palms up. They were indeed callused, the stain of too many Virginia Slims smoked into her index finger.

"My husband, he got electrocuted. Working on the powers lines over to Myrtle Beach after that big hurricane come through. You probably heard about it. Anyways, they're holding up my settlement and I gotta get some work."

"When can you start?"

"Right now." She took a long draw on her cigarette.

Wiping my hands, leaving the nettles to plot their spread, I walked her over to the apothecary garden where Lady's bedstraw romped across the cruciform paths.

"Wait here."

Crossing the bridge, a hoe under one arm, a spade across my shoulder, and a bucket holding a pair of gardening gloves dangling from my hand, I saw her toss a butt onto the gravel path and grind it under her flip-flop. I got another bucket.

"You can put your snuffed butts in this bucket. This one's for weeds. When it's full, take it over behind the barn and throw it on the compost pile. Keep this one with you. I pointed at the cigarette, then the bucket. She looked at me. Blinked, twice.

"And tomorrow, you might want to wear tennis shoes," I said.

Her look hardened. "I got to leave today at two. And I can't come tomorrow. I got court. I'll come the day after."

At quarter till two, she found me upended in a two-foot hole and handed me the bucket and tools. I struggled to my feet and walked over to the path to take a look. Three hours had netted ten feet of gravel walk, weeded. I leaned over. The tortured shreds of Lady's mantle had been wrenched off at surface level. The butt bucket lay on its side.

70

Three days later, she showed up again, and this time I demonstrated the use of spade, fork and hoe. I got the look, again. But she tried, and for three days straight, she pulled in the driveway promptly at nine, did an adequate job and left at a quarter till two.

"Another five hours," she said as she climbed behind the wheel, slammed the primered door and ground the ignition into a sputtering cough. I heard the engine smooth as she rounded the curve toward Trust.

She didn't show for a week, but one morning, fog just lifting, I heard her power steering squeal into the drive. In the passenger seat, a young woman peered through the windshield, widening her pale eyes when she saw me.

"This's my sister, Eileen." Sister's hair was a dark, muddy brown and chopped off at chin level. Pushing her bangs off her face, she nodded, her eyes the color of denim that had seen too many days in the wash.

"I got my settlement from the power company. You can work Eileen stead of me. I'll pick her up at two." And with that, Debbie sashayed back over the bridge and slid into her car.

I hadn't made it back to the potting shed when I heard an unholy scream from where I'd parked Eileen to weed a bed of tree peonies and cranesbill.

I took off across the bridge toward Sister. With a stitch in my side and a swelling stubbed toe, I gasped, "What the heck is the matter?"

She screamed again. "Snake spit! Snakes! You got snakes! You got snakes!" She began to dance around in her own pair of flip-flops, flattening a lovely bouquet of 'Johnson's Blue' Geranium.

Wondering if I'd have to administer the required slap, I maneuvered into position. Before I could corral her, she clapped a hand over her mouth and frog-sprinted toward the drive. I looked down. Spittlebugs, harmless spittlebugs, sudsing the leaves of the *Geraniums.*

We heard the gossip down at the café. Debbie had been spreading it around that I'd refused to let her use a good dose of weed-killer, and Eileen was still prostrate from the snake infestation at "that Herb of Grace place."

I shoved the Employer's Tax Guide back in the drawer. It would be a while.

Sprites and Pixies and Harvest Fairies

Three years we'd watched spring ascend the mountain, greening the trees one by one, announcing another season at The Herb of Grace. Now with just a few weeks left to hibernate, I headed south toward Betsy's Gap, a 'Perle d'Or' rose, destined for a fundraiser, resplendent in burlap and grosgrain, along for the ride. Rounding the last curve before the gap, I lowered the window, hoping to catch a whiff of the native azaleas that grew there and heard the sound of hammers and saws, a drill. More changes coming to our slice of the mountains.

Down at the café, speculation ran rampant and colorful – "a commune for some of those airy-fairy new agers" drew snorts of derision; "a loading dock for Christmas trees" lifted eyebrows; "Nah, I heard it was a spa," stifled giggles.

The real story arrived one afternoon riding in an SUV, bearing Ohio plates. From their vehicle, Jo sprang, beaming, Alf climbed, smiling. They introduced themselves as the owners of the new Mountain Inn Bed and Breakfast up at the Gap.

"We've been meaning to come down before, but we've had guests since day one," Jo said.

"Wow," I said and after a twinge of envy, really did mean it. She proved to be all that I was not – extrovert, joiner of organizations, networker of crowds, someone with connections long before the world became connected. And she wanted us to partner our businesses. I said, "Yes, oh yes. And we have to talk to Callie and Hope at Summer's Day."

From the first, Callie reminded me of a pixie, a Rackham illustration come to life. Her hair, chopped as if by an errant child, and her eyes, lined and shadowed in midnight kohl, lent her a sense of other-worldliness in a land of earth mothers. Her daughter, Hope, a hard-headed realist, tethered her flighty mother to solid ground.

Together, they opened a craft store, Summer's Day, in an old converted gas station, crowding the highway across the creek from their farmhouse. They painted the original grease-stained counter a duck egg blue, hung gingham curtains, pulled up rockers, hung shelves and filled them with Callie's hand-made dolls and Hope's jewelry. Jams, candy, bread, her own or our neighbors', lined the shelves. Out front the old Esso sign still hung. The screen door whapped a satisfactory slap upon your arrival, and Hope in her wheelchair greeted you with her smile.

On their closing days, they loved to visit us at The Herb of Grace. Pulling her Subaru around back to the kitchen, right up to the door, Callie would lean over, lift her daughter from the backseat, carry her inside, and with such tenderness, gentle her

74

onto a chair. Hope weighed maybe half her mother's 115 pounds.

I learned their story over time, revealed as most stories are during getting acquainted conversations. Hope was born during that season of joyful beginnings with brittle bone disease, osteogenesis imperfecta. No one knew. Tiny Hope would scream in pain. Her mother would rush her to the doctor. Only after her child was taken from her did the doctors discover the baby's fractures resulted from her disease and not by her mother's hand.

Hope had already outlived the predictions by the time we helped celebrate her 18th birthday and her high school graduation down at the café. Neighbors, friends, customers, and folks just traveling through gathered around tables laden with Pasta Florentine, Hope's favorite, and platters of freshly hooked trout – fried and blackened – sides of hush puppies and fries; and for those who preferred grease-dripping, mustard-dropping cheeseburgers.

Toasting her with her first taste of champagne, we all watched as Hope grinned, threw back the glass, and then held it high for another. I noticed the tremor in her hands. So did Callie, her smile dimmed by the shadow in her eyes.

The feeding frenzy that embroils the garden world in spring had receded and left us stranded in the retail desert of mid-summer, Callie wandering it with us. A call from Jo at the B&B alerted us that she had suffered her first ever vacancy the night before. We agreed to meet for coffee at the café and toss around a few marketing strategies.

Jo, flicking a morsel of fried okra in her mouth, said, "You know, there are a lot of talented people hiding back in the coves here along the creek.

"Did you know Louise and her husband make fiber art?" Jo asked.

"Yeah, and how about Judy. She's a potter, isn't she? And then there's Gabriel and his stained glass," I said.

"Ella's grape-vine baskets. Charlie's brooms."

"Denny, the story-teller!" Callie set her own mug on the table, slid into a chair.

From the kitchen redolent of bacon and biscuits, Sam joined in, "How about Joe's fountains?"

And that's how the first Herb of Grace Harvest Faire sprouted from a tiny summer-sown seed into a full-blown, leaf-turning fall celebration.

October in the Appalachians is a time of chilled-wine breezes and jewel-woven tapestries, a yin and yang of exhilaration and melancholy. Awash in this essence of autumn, we were preparing for opening day of the first, hope to be annual, Harvest Faire. The grass paths in the garden glistened emerald even under a light dusting of snow, and the 'Braithwaite' rose had surprised us with a burlesque of blooms.

The garden had become a changeling, the backdrop for troubadours, minstrels, and clowns – an assemblage of artists and their wares. Tapestries, table runners, woven on a handloom using yarn the colors of an autumn sunset, a forested glen hung on easels. Earthen vessels - pottery jostling upon a table beneath the maples. Bowls, buckets made from burl wood climbed the steps. A carnival of jewelry swung from a display made of twigs. There were booksellers, storytellers, soap makers. And being passed out through our kitchen window, Sam's artistry of hot potato soup and chili.

And now Kim's contribution - designing flyers, tapping customer lists, releasing press releases in all the surrounding newspapers - was bearing fruit. In cars and vans, on bicycles and even one on horseback, a whole host of revelers, shoppers, and those who just wondered, "What the hell are they up to now?" poured across our gated thresholds.

People stood wall to wall in the front room of the shop, all 150 square feet of it. John stood at the door greeting all who entered with the bonhomie of a superb host or a really good hotel concierge. Outside, Kim herded a gaggle of voyeurs through the gardens. Me? I was playing the proverbial chicken without its head, scurrying one way and then another, trying to take care of all the chicks and customers.

I'm trying to ring up a dozen tins of cooking herbs for a couple while a woman, hovering over the counter, fiddling a four-inch herb pot in front of my face is asking, "How big will this fennel grow?"

At the same time, the woman behind her asks, "How do I not kill this lavender?" The receipt for the herbs is hanging from my fingers, my mouth hanging open, when a fairy-sized, black-haired woman-child, conjured straight from Middle Earth, materializes at my elbow and begins to bag the customer's purchases.

Throughout the afternoon, she seemed to pop up wherever most needed – ladling soup, directing traffic, or simply listening. The sun was spreading its jewel-like glow over our valley as the last stragglers left. We shut the gate behind them, and I turned to our worker angel and asked. "Who are you?"

"I'm Maree. Jo invited me. Thought I'd stay. See if you needed help." It seemed the most natural thing in the world as I reached to hug her, and she hugged me back.

"Thank you."

And that's how we met Maree. Throughout the years to follow, she wove her spirit into all our lives – became helper, friend, famiy.

Farther Afield

A Blade of Quaking Grass in a Field of Lilies

Though grateful to a fellow nurseryman and seasoned lecturer for suggesting me as a speaker, I looked over the Garden Club audience from the lecturers' table, feeling as queasy as a fledgling peering from its nest. This was the first time I'd faced a crowd with nothing but words and a few measly props since I'd prayed for deliverance in a high school speech class.

As Daniel, nurseryman and deliverer of innocent lambs, dipped oyster shell into a bucket of potting soil in preparation for his presentation on growing herbs in pots, I looked around the cabin. Sunlight slanted through a window onto the walls, planked in knotty pine. A breeze stirred the curtains, releasing the aroma of campfires or, I gave another sniff, like the fragrance stirring in the shadows of the empty smokehouse at my grandparents' Alabama farm. A homey smell. I could do this.

But as Daniel passed along practical tips on protecting lavender leaves from soil splashback and pruning rosemary often – sounding downright professorial – my confidence in the program I'd mulled over, planned, listed, categorized, polished over the past month appeared now a pitiful thing.

From where I sat, I couldn't see a single set of dirt-grimed fingernails or weather-swollen knuckles or calluses, unlike me. Everyone looked poised down to their elegantly crossed ankles – my Lord – all of them pointed in the same direction, like debutantes at the cotillion.

Looking down at the ivory-colored parchment atop my notes, I rubbed my fingers across the pastels, coloring my hand rendered sketch. Down at Office Depot I'd paid for twenty-five color copies to share with the club participants. A talk on the history and use of each plant in the drawing was to fill my allotted time. As inspiration for the garden plan, I had read, again, from the lovely book by Elizabeth Goudge, *The White Witch* – an elder tree by a well, rosemary by the front door, a path hedged in lavender, a parterre of *Germander*, and inside sops-in-wine, paggles, gilliflowers, love-lies-bleeding, well bleeding over a paling fence, and sage tempering the exuberance of comfrey. Last night I felt pretty good about my presentation. Now, eyes roving over the impeccably coifed women and solitary male who, no doubt, employed their assembled gardening fingers to direct the help, I felt my heart flutter and my cheeks flame rose red. Dropping my head, hiding behind the pretense of consulting my notes, I – wait a minute. Was that a smudge? Smears like a little kid's failure to paint inside the lines? My stomach clenched, and then I remembered. My smart looking easel with its accompanying flip chart bar and tacks and post-its still leaned against a stack of one-gallon black plant pots just outside the potting shed, forgotten.

On the way to the podium, I stumbled, scattering the contents of my cracked faux leather folio across the polished floor. Several spectators scrambled to help me gather the heel-smudged pages. I stuffed them, creased and out of order, back into the binder and turned to face the music. As I opened my mouth to greet the crowd, my lips stuck - like tongue to ice cube - to my teeth. To this day I don't remember what I said or the response I received. But for years afterward, two of the stalwarts from that day of personal torment, perpetual cotillion attendees still - Emma of the sky-blue eyes and Helen of the rich-girl hair - came to tea once a month and bought herbs and roses for their garden.

Maiden Voyage to the Circus of Herbal Delights

Almost midnight and we were still packing. The peepers had fallen silent in the pools and woods beyond our feeble porch light, and the stars were scattering miracles across the ocean of night overhead. The dying beam from my flashlight ferreted out a little space between the stack of soaps and tins and the pile of baskets and linens. I passed John the bags of dried herbs I'd darted back inside to retrieve. I kept thinking of things to take with us, my weariness playing fool with all my bright ideas. We didn't need two inspiration stones bearing the message "Happy." And with everything I added, John had to rearrange and restack, dawn creeping ever closer. Feeling our way through unlit greenhouses, we fumbled for flats of lavenders and rosemaries, thymes and sages, pots of old roses and vines and perennials. Trusting that my nose and fingertips would recognize one variety from another, their shadows offering only a hint to their identities, I passed tray after tray to John, who in turn stuffed them onto makeshift shelves slotted into the back of our Subaru station wagon. This was our second load headed over the mountain to Asheville and our first ever Herb Festival.

We had no idea what to expect. Joining the local branch of the North Carolina Herb Association back in the fall seemed like a good way to become involved, garner knowledge and contacts, and be able to participate in what we were told was "a real money maker." Started as a local spring get-together, the show had grown, drawing vendors and shoppers from as far away as Alabama and Arkansas. So here we were, the sun just teasing out the morning, backed up to our 10-foot by 18-foot half-bay that now looked to my sobered eyes like a vast, empty warehouse. And it was as cold as that proverbial well-digger in the Klondike. As a nursery friend told us, you can't depend on spring in the mountains until Mother's Day. I knew our meager wares would huddle, like us, lost and cold in the emptiness.

We set up our two tables – one cheap folding, the other a find from my former South Carolina barn – and I slung a blue checked oilcloth over them to hide a kaleidoscope of vintage paint spatter. An old door set on sawhorses played counter for shop stuff. Covered in the antique Battenburg tablecloth I'd been hauling around from one life to another since Kim's childhood; the makeshift arrangement looked to me more like a sow's ear dressed up like a lacy demilune than I'd hoped. Johnny Jump-Ups, Viola tricolor, strutted across the surface where I'd scattered them, bumping up against French soaps, herbal lotions and books. Our tin cash box, full of hopeful change, sat to the back next to a hand-held calculator.

We were still fiddling, dragging thymes forward, shoving lavenders to the rear, when the first customers began to mill around. Only then did we look at our neighbors. In the next booth and continuing down the line in both directions stood professional plant tables and ramshackle plant tables, all bare and unadorned except for regimented rows of little black pots and little green leafy arms waving in the breeze. I prayed for a hole to swallow us up, hiding me and my gussied-up little booth all tarted up for the fair.

A Day at the Circus – Year Two

Birds rustled in the trees, still too rumpled and sleepy to sing, as we rose for our second year as vendors at the annual Herb Festival. By this time, John had acquired a used camper shell for the Ford F-250 and built shelves around the sides. We'd loaded until ten the night before with the stars lighting the hoop houses. Out at the rose beds, 'Dainty Bess' looked quite fetching, all budded and blooming, as was 'Sweet Juliet'. Demure 'Louise Odier' sighed alongside a boisterous 'L.D. Braithwaite'. In the *Clematis* house, a ruby red 'Niobe' crooked a tendril my way while 'Elsa Spath' waved from mid-row. I had embraced them all and more as I carried them to the truck.

At first light, we opened the camper to an assault of scent so palpable you could taste it – a slurp of golden nectar. Dawn showed up in an apricot wonder of low lying clouds and periwinkle sky – worth every backbreaking stoop, every stubbed toe, every bloody finger of the past weeks and months. And yes, inside the Subaru, antique linens, lavender, rose and fig soaps, and creams and books, snuggled up together eager for their ride to town. A trio of birds and rabbits from an ironmonger's studio, secreted in his suburban Georgia garage, hugged the wheel well. I'd thought about just shoving in my little black pots, resplendent enough in their spring green, but I had decided to adopt my unrepentant, black sheep Auntie's lifetime philosophy, being if you've already hung it all out for the world to see, don't be backing down now.

We approached the long row of produce sheds on the lookout for our assigned booth. Pride of place had been awarded once again to the "Herbe Shoppe." But, Lord have Mercy, there we were only two booths down, between "Good Plants" with their envy-provoking logoed vans and "Herb's Herbs," the nursery belonging to the president of the association. And look at that. This year, "Plants" professionally elevated tables sported an array of glazed pots front and center. And Herb had set his cash register on top of a pink chintz tablecloth.

We were amazed that day. Plant-hungry crowds, stroking rosemaries, sniffing mints, smearing creams, held sweet lace linens up to the sun. In that heyday of all things gardening, the enthusiasts, eager to learn the biology, the history and the uses of plants, queued up, all yearning to make a garden.

Alas, lest I formed an opinion of myself above my potential (i.e., get too big for my britches), a neighboring vendor, swaddled in quilt remnants and Mardi Gras beads, provided a reality check. Swinging through my displays with obvious contempt, she announced, "This festival is being ruined by newbies who don't know the proper way to do things."

She walked back to her booth, slapped a hand down on a pile of yard sale rugs and began to shift them from one table to another, all the better to highlight her mayonnaise-jarred creams and broken glass baubles. I remained chastened.

The First (and Last) Summer Solstice Faire

John called them my brain-hitches. Kim just rolled her eyes, knowing she'd be suckered into bailing out Mama again. I called them moments of panic, products of slow weeks when customers kept their hands and their money in their pockets.

I'd commandeered Maree, too, for the day of our first "Summer Solstice Faire," in honor of, well actually because of, a troop of Girl Scouts out of Greenville, South Carolina that wanted to come for a field trip on the 21st day of June. The leader had seen a mention of The Herb of Grace in an article by a local newspaper columnist. "We need a program. You'll figure it out," she said.

The day arrived with an air of festival - golden sunshine, summer-laden breeze, and a sky devoid of looming portent. Too warm for a fire in the ceremonial cauldron - syrup kettle in its everyday life - even if I'd been foolish enough to light one. Host to a refreshment table, a canvas gazebo shared the garden with herb filled baskets, flower burdened trugs, stools, chairs, and the cauldron.

Two mini vans drove up, disgorging fourteen scouts, a dozen assorted younger siblings, and a swarming hive of adult leaders and chaperones, before they'd come to a full stop. I directed the jamboree across the garden and down the stone steps, descending a hill swimming with *Geranium* 'Lawrence Flatman' to the site of the festivities. Since none of the kids seemed to be familiar with the practice of follow the leader or "one at a time!" the 'Lawrences' sea of small striated faces fell victim to an army of trampling Keds.

As soon as they spotted the cauldron, the girls squealed and started dancing around it to the tune of "Shake, Shake, Shake your Booty." Every time they shouted the word booty, they'd execute a kick, catching their younger siblings on their vulnerable backsides.

Calling order by jumping in front of the ring leader, I pointed them to the basket where Maree started passing out fronds of 'Silver King' *Artemisia*, lavender, and *Santolina* to weave into fairy crowns. Appropriating all the silver, green and gray herbs, a mafia of older scouts began plaiting and poking them into stiff little circles, then jamming them over the heads of the lower ranks who hovered in terror. Oblivious, leaders and chaperones had bellied up to the tables, grazing and chewing the gossip cud, snapping their fingers for refills.

I looked at Kim. She looked at Maree. Maree looked at me. I sighed. No longer my mother's world, or mine, this Solstice looked like being a long one.

What was to have been a simple snack, "Oh we'll feed the girls before we come," turned out to be an emptying of cupboards, even down to our personal granola disguised as "fairy grain," to feed the grumbling herd.

My marketing plan had been to lure the adults into a little shopping, while their young charges floated about the garden on the lookout for fairies. Displayed around the cauldron on varnished tree stumps, draped tables, old wheelbarrows, I'd staged my most beguiling plants, the most seductive toiletries, the most interesting books. As they plowed past on their rush to the grub, no one spared a glance their way. The third attempt by an older scout to toss a brownie into the kettle destroyed the last of the displays.

As dusk fell, I counted the losses and checked "Summer Solstice Faire" off my list of marketing strategies. With the leavings of the pink fairy juice, Kim toasted my decision.

We add a ... Tearoom?

Shrouded beneath the branches of an old maple, twisted and hollowed with age, the first tearoom at The Herb of Grace sat carpeted in jewel-like moss and draped in hellebores and *Hydrangeas*. Necessity being blessed in its search for invention.

Twilight hung in the sky, reluctant to leave us. In the soft light, the car pulling away and up the mountain hesitated as if it, too, hated to go; the people inside waving, hands ghost-like against the darkening day. Drained, I looked at my watch – eight o'clock, two hours past closing. In my apron pocket, a five and a one rubbed alongside a couple of quarters. I sighed. Three hours, two plants.

Shoulders aching, feet burning, stomach growling – oh for Scarlett's cold turnip – I started up the steps, bent like an old rake. From somewhere, I heard the ringing of a telephone, the one discarded and forgotten, no doubt, at some point on this endless day. I finally unearthed it from underneath a stack of baskets on the sales porch, still ringing. Unbelievable.

"Hello." Over at the barn the bats darted and circled, finding their way home. "Hello?"

"Hello." In the background, a radio played, "... you can start to make it better." Hey Jude?

"Is this the Herb of Grace?"

"Yes, it is. Sorry, I was about to close and I..."

"Oh. I'm sorry. I'll call back. I didn't mean... I'm sorry. I'll go."

I thought of the six dollars, the two quarters. "No, wait, it's all right. Please. What can I do for you?"

She asked if we served tea. She'd heard of us, and her granddaughter was coming all the way from Michigan, and her friend spoke so enthusiastically about her visit, and, really, she wanted it to be special for her, Abby that is, who'd just graduated from high school, and, well it had been a rough few years for her, Abby, what with her step-mother and all, and she, the grandmother, would so love to do tea.

And I said, "Yes." To my surprise. Of course I would. So on that next Saturday, The Herb of Grace held its first ever tea. And it felt right. Slipping in, just like that, to complete a dream only half-formed, or as John put it, half-baked.

The morning bloomed cool and fragrant, almost liquid, as if you stuck out your tongue, it would taste like a mint julep. I stopped half way between the kitchen and the barn, inhaling the richness of green mountain air and black coffee, then felt time tick over and pick up speed.

Out at the barn, the last of the bats were arriving, fanning the air in their haste for sleep. Behind the tractor, I found the card table, hauled it out and then drug-stepped it over the bridge to the old maple. I set it up ankle-deep in a bed of *Pulmonaria*. It wiggled. I moved it onto the moss – still wiggled. Pushing it down, I administered my own wiggle. It listed to port. It needed a good chock. Rocks are plentiful in the mountains and after a few tries, I found the perfect three to level the table.

Back inside, I gathered the players and props for this first production, this tea. Emulating, remembering all those impromptu tea parties I'd held – little tomboy in her bare feet and jeans, pinkie finger held aloft. Stepping into the front room of the shop, I lifted a vintage teapot from the English cupboard, slipped off the price tag. Fired a pure white porcelain and fat like a cabbage, the teapot was a bit of a mongrel, but I loved it. I placed it in the wicker basket with a pair of mismatched Wedgwood cups and saucers and damask napkins worn smooth by many hands.

Outside, the Lady's Mantle had shaken off its pearled dew, and thin clouds combed a blue sky. I draped a remnant over the table, just a scrap really, from a bride's trousseau – Battenberg lace, folded many times into a trunk of memories. It floated to the ground, hiding the humble identity of the table and its trio of rocks. I thought about the antique shop, little bigger than the Lion's wardrobe, piled high with old linens, where I found the remnant, a four-year-old Kim snuggled up against me. It was all we bought that day, a piece of someone's memory being all we could afford.

Back in the kitchen, I sliced melon and Gouda cheese, then chopped tomatoes from our garden, snipped fresh basil over them and drizzled balsamic vinegar and olive oil over the top. As they marinated, I set the bread in the oven for its last rise. Next, I mixed the batter for scones, adding a smidgen of brown sugar. I'd serve them with fresh whipped cream and

Mom's strawberry jam. I robbed the shop, again, for a box of Darjeeling and an infuser shaped like a dollhouse.

They arrived late, Mrs. Adler and Abby, looking a little green, a hazard of the winding road. Different than I'd envisioned from the halting, tentative voice over the phone. Almost intimidating, the grandmother was tall and elegant and slender. But Abby seemed to shrink, an apology to the world that held no place for her. When I said "hello," she shied like a frightened colt. Oh Lord, I didn't want to fail for so many reasons. This child being one of them.

Then Mrs. Adler introduced her, "This is Abby, my granddaughter." And I heard Love made audible.

I escorted them down the steps and seated them at the table. As I poured their first cup of tea, a cloud passed over the sun, moved on. I released a held breath and climbed back up the steps for the fruit and cheese and bruschetta. As I placed them center stage, wind stirred the leaves overhead, garnishing the fruit with twigs and debris.

As I presented to the table a small dish – flow-blue swimming through porcelain – filled with jam and cream, thunder rattled the ground. As I set the scones to rest upon the table, from the mountain above came the sounds of a legion on the move. I grabbed the teapot, whipped the scones and jam off the table and sprinted to the shop. The rain reached us just as Abby clutched her grandmother's hand and fled, following me up the steps. Behind me, I heard a whoop of laughter.

They finished their tea on the shop's narrow porch, surrounded by pots of herbs and old baskets, holding their plates in their laps. I heard Abby say, "This is fun," as she reached for another scone.

Mrs. Adler admitted, "I've never actually been to a tea."

I marveled. Her manners had seemed impeccable as if schooled in the art of taking tea. It was only as she reached for the teapot to be "mother" and pour the hot China tea that I noticed her hands. Callused, the knuckles large and swollen as only hard work could make them. They looked like mine.

"That's okay," I said. "I've never actually served a tea before."

Years later, sitting on the wide expanse of the Verandah, the grandmother and I, old comrades by then, laughed about that first tea as she and her newly-betrothed granddaughter sipped hot China tea, and the rain fell in torrents off the roof.

Loaves and Fishes

Since that first tea party, the garden beneath the old maple had held court to herb aficionados, old rose wranglers, courting couples, and friends. When the program director for the Hoer's Garden Club out of Franklin called to reserve tea, the sun was shining, the birds were singing, and the creek tinkled. All was right with our world, so, of course, I gave a resounding "yes!"

"How many?" I asked.

"Twelve have signed up so far. There's a couple who haven't responded yet."

We agreed on a Friday, three weeks away.

A week later, birds still singing, I picked up the phone.

"Hello."

"Hi, this is Dee, one of the Hoer's. I'm calling with an updated number. Three more have said yes and two of the original twelve have invited friends."

The end of the month loomed. I pulled out the menu, studied it, crossed out rustic vegetable tart and wrote quiche. I could use a piecrust mix. I kept to the French Tart, but added a double-chocolate gateau.

Another week passed. A bird or two peeped, the creek more rumbling than tinkling, when I answered the ring.

"Hi, Dee here. Friends have added friends and we're up to twenty-five."

I could stretch the quiches if I added a simple tomato wine soup. I totted numbers in my head – more bread, more teacakes, more fruit, more cheese.

I called Kim in Atlanta. "Honey, can you pay Mom a visit." I think she sensed my rising panic. She said yes.

It was still dark outside when I left the bed, stumbled into the kitchen. I'd baked the desserts the day before. Baked the French loafs. Whipped the quiche filling. I'd timed the assembly and the soup to be served piping hot. Right now, I needed to wake up and then slice the cheeses – a Gouda, a farmer's, and a brie; the fruit – grapes, melon, and kiwi. I looked at the clock, fogged from my steaming cuppa. Kim should arrive by eleven. Plenty of time to cover the tables, set them, and decorate. The folding tables had been leaning against the maple since John and I had groped our way down the unlighted steps sometime around midnight.

I raised my head from the mound of melon on the cutting board. Dawn appeared to be slow in coming – silence from the heavens, in the trees. The creek growled.

Kim pulled in as the first warning drops fell. By the time she reached the back door, the rain sheeted. We grabbed raincoats, slid down the slope to the maple, and proceeded to manhandle five borrowed card tables and two garden tables back up the steps, around the house and into the kitchen – the only room big enough to accommodate twenty-five garden clubbers. Setting them up in the kitchen, drying them off, mopping the puddles off the floor, placing the settings happened in a bit of a mental fog.

Kim was placing the last tier on the last table as the bus – bus! – pulled in. We started counting, ten, fifteen, twenty, twenty-five, thirty, thirty-five. Forty-one women trailed into the kitchen, hats molting, to sit at tables, lace covered TV trays and a bedside table draped in a damask sheet.

We've talked since, Kim and me. All we can remember of that "tea" is sidestepping each other, bumping into counters, weaving through gossiping, laughing women. Tray after tray of bread, bowl after bowl of infusions, and enough tomato wine soup to float a boat or sink a ship. As they trailed down the garden path, heels slapping through puddles, the sun popped out from behind a cloud, thrushes orchestrated a chorale, and the creek rippled gaily.

The thank you note we received read, "...Loved everything!" and it bore forty-one signatures.

Meanwhile...

Back at the Shop

A Circle of Three

They stepped through the door laughing, the three of them, bringing in the scent of rain.

"We just made it!" one said.

And sure enough, at their backs, lightning flashed and thunder rumbled the windows. Wearing sundresses in prism colors - purple, opal, and aquamarine - carrying small packages wrapped in tissue paper, they appeared ready to celebrate. Looking like a tidy flock of Gouldian Finches, busily chirping among themselves, they spied the corner cupboard first. Standing open, it held laced-edged runners, embroidered tea towels, and handkerchiefs of the most delicate gossamer, all folded and held in place by sprigs of lavender. Tucked in next to the tea towels, a tarnished silver goblet held a tiny bird's nest woven of vines and thistle down. In the nest lay a single glass egg the color of blood roses.

"Ooh," sighed one of the women as she reached for it, turned to the woman next to her, held out the goblet and toasted, "Happy birthday!"

Three friends, neighbors south of the French Broad and members of the same garden club where I'd presented my shaky maiden talk. They had remembered me - Anne, Barbra, and birthday Julia - and heard about our diminutive shop library. Could they hold their impromptu party there, please?

I carried a café chair from the porch to join the two already sitting by the window, between them a wicker stool for a table. Five minutes later, I carried in a steaming pot of Oolong, teacakes on a plate of violet and pots of cream and jam and deposited the tray, my contribution to the festivities.

They settled in, around them gardening friends - Gertrude Jekyll at Munstead Wood, Vita at Sissinghirst, Christo and Beatrix - whose dust jackets were as colorful as these companions' party frocks, waited to listen in and share their stories. Curious as I was, I left them to it.

Back up the hall in the front room of the shop, I moved a tulip-shaped teapot, sprouting its own porcelain bloom, from a table to the empty spot left by the goblet. At one point, I stepped outside and hauled trays of herbs and pots of roses and lavender decorating the porch down to the sidewalk and into the rain. Bending over, I watched as raindrops beaded the Lady's Mantle hugging the walkway. Each leaf held a jewel of water at its heart, nature making my efforts feel like gilding the lily.

Every so often, I'd return to the library to replenish their tea. One pour interrupted a snort of laughter, another tears. An hour turned into two, and I thought they must be getting hungry for more than teacakes, so I crept to the kitchen, sliced a half baguette of bread, warmed a ramekin of olive oil, a clove of Italian garlic and a twig of 'Tuscan Blue' rosemary, sliced a round of Gouda and arranged the peasant's supper on a white platter. As I passed the refrigerator, I grabbed a pod of green grapes and set them next to the cheese. When I entered the room, Anne whooped her thanks. For a while, I heard only the sounds of breaking bread.

The afternoon slipped away, customers and passersby discouraged by the sodden day. I tweaked the jewelry display, shuffled baskets, brought the plants back up onto the porch, pushed pots around, even dusted corners and polished windows. At last, the clouds slid off the ridge top, thinned to expose the day's last wash of sunlight. At ten minutes past closing time, I heard stirring in the library.

"We've had the best time today," Anne said as she walked toward me, stopping in the doorway.

"Oh, yes," Barbra agreed and nudged around her.

"Thank you for making my birthday so special. I needed this. I turned fifty today. And yesterday, I buried a long dead marriage. Thank God!" From the hallway Julia's laughter sounded like loss and liberation.

Their car pulled onto the road, heading up the mountain, hands waving out the windows. I waved back, then shut the door and locked it. Back in the library, the wicker table was once again a stool, the tray, the platter, the cups, the saucers all stacked and waiting just outside the kitchen door.

Portents

The dog days of summer arrived and hung on, stagnating every waking hour, refusing to loosen its grip and surrender at last to autumn. I woke up that Saturday, already weary. As I dropped the curtain over the screen door divider between the kitchen and the shop's gallery hall and hung the "private" sign, I felt a Macbethian pricking of my thumbs, the day already seeming to seethe with foul portent.

On my way down the hall, I tripped over the box of frescoes I'd set in the doorway so I wouldn't forget to hang them. My creations from the winter past spent spring and summer languishing beneath the bed, joining other boxes of bags and goods in temporary storage – years long. It took until this September day to convince myself that they might be good enough, maybe, to join other artisan's wares in the shop. I lined them along a windowsill – an iris and stone, a rose and arbor, an ivy over a wall, and a topiary beneath the beams of an old stable aglow in a ray of sunshine – all about the size of a book cover.

Outside under a maudlin sky, a car horn blared, held down by an impatient hand. I unlocked the door, opened it. Peered out. The horn, again. Crossing the porch, I descended the steps to another blast from the horn, passed through the arbor and came face to grill with a Honda Accord, climbing the sidewalk, hood kissing the privacy fence, engine running. I could see the two women sitting there, so I smiled, nodded. A minute passed. Stepping closer, I leaned over and knocked on the driver's side window. Overhead, a Cardinal chirped, once, as if another peep would constitute more than this muggy morning warranted. I stepped back. The window slid down a few inches, stopped, then stuttered a few more.

Turning her head of silvered curls, the driver looked at me with the haughtiness of the committee chair, the superiority of the flower show judge, the disdain of the club president emeritus evident in every breath she took before saying, "Is this it? Are you open? Well?" The passenger, like Lot's wife, never moved, staring straight ahead, stuck to her seat by well-trained obedience or fear, awaiting her command to "Fetch."

Weariness, my old friend, climbed back up the steps with me, followed by the sound of car doors opening and the fluted notes of "Look at that 'Nelly Moser'. Can't hold a candle to mine."

Usually a good month, September, lacking the frenzy of spring or the leaf-worshipping furies to come, it instead offered a cheerful, sedate parade of gardening customers. But the auguries had escaped and mayhem was afoot. On the heels of the ladies who maligned my 'Nelly', a van with Florida plates and a Volusia County sticker, pulled in next to the Accord and disgorged a clutch of AARP members.

109

"Okay! Listen up! Twenty minutes! Do I hear it!" The acting tour guide cupped his ear, hooted again, "Twenty minutes!" Raising a finger in the air, twirling it clockwise, then counter, he – I'm not making this up – blew his whistle. Like good little t-shirted (Winnebago logo), cargo-shorted (L.L. Bean), walking shoe-shod (New Balance) minions, the three couples and his (I assume) wife, quick stepped onto the porch and into the shop. I walked in behind them. The line to the restroom snaked down the hall.

One little rebel did score a bar of fig soap and a lavender sachet under the vigilant eye of the timekeeper before they sped away down the hill toward the Chapel (ten minutes) and a bite to eat (half an hour) at the Creek Café.

I closed my eyes, waiting for the next episode.

"Do you ever make a dime way out here?" I looked over at the man standing next to the counter. I get asked this question, or variations thereof, more than my good mannered upbringing would have expected, the boors running to a type – usually male, in his fifties, or older, usually one of a coed duo, and fancies himself the comedic spokesman for any group he can persuade to include him. I smiled at this one as I've learned to do, imagining him having to buy a friend.

I leave them, his wife circling the shop, to greet a dear friend and customer, blown in on a kind wind. In his eighties, Mr. Barusky spent his youth in Nazi Germany, escaping to Canada ahead of the internment trains. Honorable, courtly, with impeccable manners, he has a beautiful smile. Today he'd come for a rosemary, a replacement for the one his cat mangled.

Another gentleman joined us among the 4-inch herb pots. With his buzz cut and camo, he looked like he rode around with a deer strapped to his hood, but my assessment took a swift kick when he said, "Cooking is my passion." He wanted to know how to use his sage. Lifting it, he gave the pot a twirl, then nodded at the rosemary in his other hand, dipping it in a little herbal curtsey.

"How about with venison stew?" he asked, and I could feel an adjustment to my assumptions, a broadening of my horizons.

"Hold on." I walked into the shop, avoiding eye contact with the rude arrival, now the rooted center to his revolving wife. The ladies in the Accord must have been in the library, critiquing my collection of books.

Back out on the porch, I handed our hunter-gatherer one of our culinary herb charts. He beamed as if I'd awarded him his first Michelin star. "Let me get you both a cup of tea. Just sit." I left my friend and the cook fondling the plants as if they couldn't decide what to name them.

In the kitchen, I set the kettle on to boil and took a deep breath. It felt like a green gunpowder moment. I reached for the tea and a pot, filled the infuser and let my mind idle. Out in the hall, I heard a scrape, then a rattle. I looked over at the privacy door and dropped my eyes to where the curtain ended a foot or so from the floor – two upended faces bobbing up against the screen and their four piggy eyes peering through. I

111

raised my eyebrows, pursed my lips; I could only imagine the view from the other side. I heard a clunk like someone's head ricocheting off a plaster wall, then a scuttle. By the time I reached the porch with the tea, their opinionated backsides were down the steps and sliding onto the front seat of their waiting Accord.

And the funny man concerned for my economic welfare? His wife bought two of the frescoes, a book on French tea, and a jar of lavender honey, all for a bit more than a ten-cent piece.

A Coven of Belonging

Kim's latest press release to the Asheville Citizen-Times had customers and the curious jostling elbow to elbow in our little two-room shop. Granted that amounted to no more than a fat dozen, but it felt good. Replenishing culinary herbs from supplies stored in the kitchen pie safe and dried roses from cartons shoved beneath the guest room bed, then trotting uphill to our small greenhouse for more potted herbs had me happy, but dragging.

They hovered just inside the door – three of them. At first glance, they seemed interchangeable, stuffed as they were into polyester print dresses, matching black tennis shoes. Instead, they came bearing their badges of individuality upon their heads – hair of a different stripe – red on black, purple on black and a modest light brown on dark. Huddling together, wary, like puppies in an unfamiliar world, they kept their backs to the wall, moving toward a display of herbal tisanes and honey.

"What's this then?" Millie had slipped through the door past the trio and was holding aloft a plant of gray-green, roughly puckered leaves.

"Costmary," I said over my shoulder.

"Bible leaf, you mean." She smirked, lifting her eyebrows at the customer standing next to her. Shouldering her aside, looking like a prize laying-hen, Millie stuck the small pot back in its place – next to an old copy of Eleanor Rohde's *A Garden of Herbs* – and bustled back out the door.

Looking after her, counting the times she'd done this pop-in during the past week, I caught sight of a red on black head of hair. As the young woman reached for a tiny stone gargoyle perched on a tin of dried marigolds, her sleeve slid up, exposing stylishly dyed underarm hair in alternating stripes of red and black.

Glancing my way, she saw my eyes shift and speared me with a triumphant, "We're witches!" scattering my other customers to the corners and out onto the porch. "Wiccans!" The puppy snapped.

Propping a fist on her hip – displaying the W-I-T-C self inked across her knuckles – she bristled, waited. It seemed churlish to tell her they weren't my first, along with one Irish Rastafarian, a couple of red-haired, sun-burned Vodoun, and a gaggle of newly minted Native Americans, all lost seekers searching for an identity of one kind or another, all traveling out from Asheville in their rusting Datsuns and vintage Peugeots.

I wanted to give them what they needed. I did. But all I could think to say on that hot, bitter summer day was, "Really?"

114

Stretching to her full five feet three inches, she spat, "Wiccan is real. A true religion." The tiny spitting gargoyle straining for help in the strangle-hold of her tightly clenched fist.

They continued to circle, stopping to inspect the beeswax candles, stir the French soaps. Rising from the bowl, the aroma of rose and fig and bamboo quickly lost ground to the earthy ripeness emanating from the three young witches. The small room was growing smaller. Back behind the counter, I shuffled the day's receipts, added them again. Grabbed a dust cloth. Dusted. Tried, again. "Are you local? Your, uh, Coven, I mean."

At that, they turned in unison, spent a few seconds just looking at me. "We do not practice the black arts. We are strictly on the side of good. All our potions and spells are for love, or friendship or, or..."

"A good harvest," I supplied.

They glared. "We should not all be persecuted, you know. Or made fun of."

"Of course not," I said.

I shut up. I was failing them miserably. In a world of indifference, they just wanted their own claim to uniqueness, as did we all. So I listened. And they talked, so earnest, like children tugging at Mama, just wanting five minutes in her spotlight.

I risked a question. "Is Wiccan in your culture? I mean, were your parents witches? How long have you been, uh, Wiccas, witches?"

115

They looked at one another, calculating. Purple on Black answered, "Oh, I think it's been well over three months."

They took turns posing for pictures with the gargoyle, sat for a while among the books. They walked the gardens, every now and then throwing their arms in the air, pirouetting in circles. They gravitated to the espalier and the young man patiently brushing sea green paint onto thirsty wooden lattice. Although he never looked their way, I saw my nephew Stephen, here for a long-distance visit, stiffen, hesitate, and then begin, once more, to paint, an embarrassment of blushes creeping up his neck, staining his ears a bright crimson. At the end of their tour, Moldora, Medea, and Morina reached out, hugged me. Taking a deep breath, I held the hug and patted their backs. Then, Moldora offered me a "talisman, you know." It looked a lot like one of the sprays of Artemisia absinthium – wormwood – I kept in a willow basket hanging from the rafters of the porch.

A Time of Fireflies

It was a summer of fourteen-hour days - fraught with too much to do and too little space to be doing it in - that last one, between the old shop and the new. Every morning I awoke to lists and chores and plants and customers - with no time to stick my head outside and just breathe in the richness of my world - too busy for memories. Except for a precious few.

Stephen, my brother's son, arrived from Arizona on the first day of June, trading in the desert landscape of Phoenix for our verdant mountains and valleys. Since he left with his folks as a toddler, I'd seen him a total of maybe twenty-two, twenty-three times - not even one for every year of his life. Sum of the days getting to know him? A hundred, maybe.

As John and I waited for Kim to bring him from the airport, I wondered how Stephen would take to our hills. At times, the silence was so profound it could have been the morning of the third day here on earth. Our way of life swung the pendulum between a maniacal circus and a circle of friends around our old fiery kettle, the night sky an explosion of stars. When Stephen stepped out of Kim's car, he looked up at the sky, the surrounding trees weeping lush and green from the rain-storm just passing through.

"Wow!" His face a study in wonder, he allowed me to hug him like he had every one of those past twenty-three visits. And then he hugged me back.

The next morning, still huddled inside his blankets, Stephen stumbled into the hallway and into our first customer of the day (an experience repeated by Niece Ingrid six weeks later), thereby altering the habit of a lifetime. Seven a.m. the next day found him in the kitchen. I poured him a cup of coffee.

His first week with us, I spent every waking moment placating customers, answering the telephone or responding to another plant or pet emergency. Stephen ate for three days on leftover macaroni and cheese from his arrival dinner, the only thing I had on hand resembling vegetarian, his diet of choice. In passing, I handed him the kitchen shears and told him to take anything out of the garden he wanted. If he harvested greens for a salad, I never noticed, caught up as I was in preparing French tarts and selling plants. Living the clichés – making hay while the sun shone; striking while the iron was hot.

One night after closing, we took him down to the café to partake in the Friday night special of fresh trout and hushpuppies. Inside, it was crowded, loud with laughter, the mouthwatering smell of fried fish, fried potatoes, fried okra hung in the air. Outside, a couple of floodlights held the night just outside the door and ushered in another carload of hungry neighbors. Our friends, Lenny and Babs, Buck and Sally, Jack and Liz scooted closer together and invited us to have a seat. As greasy napkins proliferated and fish bones piled high like Legos, Stephen smiled in bemusement, working on his second order of fries.

"Borrow the Subaru, Stephen. I'm not going anywhere." So he'd drive to Asheville, meet up with Kim and Sam, visit the revolving venues of the city to listen to a little bluegrass, a bit of jazz, a dash of the fleetingly trendy in the world of aspirations. Did he visit Biltmore? I know he made it to the Cradle of Forestry. There are pictures of him in front of the one-room schoolhouse with Kim and Sam aboard the 1914 locomotive with John. That day, I entertained a garden club from Greer, South Carolina; or did I give a talk on edible flowers? Propagated another batch of French tarragon? *Echinacea?* Feverfew? I know I baked teacakes. I was forever baking teacakes.

I'd smile at Stephen in passing, mentally wringing my hands, my brow perpetually pensive, bruised from beating myself up for neglecting him. He stood at the back door, watching me pull a sheet of pastries from the oven.

"Aunt Sue, will you, please, give me something to do?"

And that's how he ended up painting a forty-foot run of raw latticework, front and back and inside and outside, posts included. A backdrop to four espaliered, heirloom apple trees – a Cox's 'Orange Pippin', a 'Blue Pearmain', a 'Gravenstein', and a 'Roxbury Russet.' It had been standing there since the past October, growing progressively shabbier, embarrassing the young fruit trees. Stephen called it his cathedral, his life's work, one he never expected to finish. He called me Aunt Tom for a while. I called him Huckleberry.

The closing sign swung from its chain out by the road. We could hear its rhythmic creaks from our seats down below. Inside the cauldron fit for a dozen witches, a fire burned with a celebratory flame, Stephen's proclaimed cathedral finished. Not lattice, but treillage worthy of its heirloom status, now staged a production in apple trees. Night had fallen to a darkness of benevolent secrets, bringing with it a chill suggestive of childhood and ghost stories. We drew closer to the warmth.

Returning from a day in town, attracted by the flames, Jack and Cath pulled through the gate, joining the festivities. From my seat on an overturned bucket, I passed the popcorn and pointed to the cooler.

"There's beer and wine."

John brought plastic armchairs, painted the shop's iconic bubblegum purple, from the barn, our threesome becoming a circle with the addition of friends. Time ceased to be important as we caught up with the doings of the valley, moved on to the country's peccadilloes.

From across the fire pit, I watched. Cath was on a roll, roasting a couple of our county commissioners, playing off the crowd. With every rejoinder, she grew more irreverent. Stephen sat amazed at Cath's vaudeville act for the benefit of all night watchers, a look of wonder in his eyes as if he couldn't believe that his generation and ours might laugh at the same things. Not much of a talker, he made a spectacular audience.

Stories ended. The fire died to embers. Flannel shirts pulled tight against the swirling damp, we called "Good Night!" and turned homeward. From inside, a light burned – John getting ready for bed. Alongside the lattice, Stephen paused, smelling the paint, congratulating himself for a job well done. I agreed.

We turned, again, feeling our way. And then, out of the darkness, I heard a voice, reverent with wonder, Stephen asking, "What is that?" All about him were flickering points of light, floating in the night sky.

"Fireflies." I could see his face, standing close as we were, and realized, "You've never seen them before."

Apparently, he desert holds no fireflies. And I realized something else, June was ending and so was Stephen's time with us. But as we walked on, I felt humbled and blessed at being granted a glimpse of the child I'd missed.

A Guardian of Hill and Heart

The animals at The Herb of Grace held a special place in the hearts and souls of our family and friends. Some lived out the whole of their lives on the farm, several generations of hens and chicks, and Gentle Josie, our Great Pyrenees.

Because of what lurks in the dark places of a mountain farm, our Angora goats were in need of a guardian angel, and a puppy, still blinking in awe at the world she'd tumbled into, needed a job.

As a child, I'd loved a long succession of dogs. As a little girl, Kim had been herded and guarded by two great mongrels – Chris and Cedar. But this was my and John's first experience with a pedigreed, genetically programmed for duty, guard dog. So sensibly, we sought the advice of long-time owners and breeders, experts at raising working dogs. We discussed dietary and immunization requirements, training – basically, these pups are born with more common sense and innate ability than most humans – and then were instructed by everyone we consulted to take the puppy directly from her litter to her work place. "She is not a pet." We heeded the advice and she broke our hearts every night over the next few months.

When our original Angora herd of five – Mary Ann, Maisie, Kim, Sue, and Carla, named for unsuspecting family members – fell pregnant to a blue-eyed charmer, we installed a baby monitor in the barn above the kidding stalls. Mary Ann's first startled bleat crackled over the monitor at a few minutes past witching hour on a January morning knee-deep in hard-pack snow. Drained and at the end of her capricious tether, Mary Ann gave birth to Ollie Clyde – a paternal family moniker – five hours later. Exhausted she may have been, but Mary Ann snuggled little Ollie to her teat and, looking down her nose with proud disdain, shook her horns in our direction. Clearly, riff-raff was not a welcome audience to the royal first born. Diane joined the family at three a.m. the next day, followed by Ouida (my mother's name) that night at 10:45. Two weeks later, Alvina (John's mother) toppled into the world. Mothers Sue, Carla, and Kim, respectively, appeared quite willing to share their perfect little miracles with all who peered through the stable door.

This was the manger scene greeting Josie as we carried her from the pick-up to the barn for her first day on the job. She was ten weeks old. And as the babies pogo-sticked off the walls and concerned mamas bleated constantly with first-baby nerves, each Angora, young and old, took a turn, either using Josie as a launching pad or a harassed mama's butt-headed example to an unruly kid. We listened, cowering around the baby monitor, wincing at every puppy yelp, each of us trying to assure the other that this was the life she'd been born to. I still regret, all these years later, not rushing in and slugging a few goats, not snatching Josie up and racing back to cuddle her on my lap in a nice warm kitchen.

But she learned, bided her time, inflicted her first dose of discipline. After that, No One rousted Josie. Top dog, top goat, queen of all she surveyed, she loved her job and took it seriously. All was safe with Josie on her hill.

She loved and ruled us all, goats and humans alike, but she had only one true buddy – a big-eyed, lion-pawed, dignified kitten we named Spencer, who almost wasn't.

Fear and Trembling

It was during that summer of transition, the last in the old shop, after Stephen had left us to journey toward his next adventure in Chapel Hill, and our niece, Ingrid, traveled from Toronto south to our mountains. She and I were testing recipes on a Monday. Tired of interminable batches of asparagus spread, I was trying a pâté using bottled artichokes. It tasted of nothing much, just kind of mushy in the mouth. I added a smidgen of dried French thyme. Gritty mush.

It needed zip, and the zippiest ingredient in the cupboard was a bottle of schnapps, so we loaded ourselves into the Subaru for a run down the hill to Trust and the general store.

It was one of those summer days when a breeze blew off the mountain all day, and clouds dodged the sun. The front porch of the store was rocking with old men who'd hung their last tobacco, raised their last cane a decade ago. A couple of their women-folk, idle for the first time that day, sat apart. We exchanged howdies, and they went back to rocking, sizing up something that lay under the bait box.

Inside, Ingrid headed to the dipped ice cream while I checked out the condiment offerings – Texas Pete and a single dusty packet of McCormick's Original Chili Mix. I grabbed the Pete and walked it to the counter where Kay minded the till. We traded pleasantries and a little light-hearted gossip. "What are they all looking at?" I asked, nodding toward the porch.

Kay wrinkled her nose. "Something dead, I think."

Back out on the porch, Ingrid and I spotted it.

"Car hit it. Just kept on a going." The row of heads doddled up and down, up again. Pushing back his John Deere cap, stiffened by decades of sweat and tractor grease, their self-designated spokesman nodded – up, down – repeated. "Just kept on a going."

Kneeling down, we peered under the depository of worms and crickets. The tiny kitten lay so very still, charcoal gray head against pocked black asphalt, eyes hidden between white paws, as if it had been saying its nightly prayers. Ingrid reached out a finger just as the little fella lifted a smudged face, white mask, coal-black cheeks, and heartrending eyes. Mirrored by the pleading eyes, Ingrid turned to me.

He rode home in her lap, not moving, and I thought the effort of lifting his head had been a final plea, his last. She carried him close to her face, cradled against her chest.

"Is he breathing?" I asked as we turned in the drive, crossed the run-off and idled as close to the kitchen door as I could get.

"I think so."

UPS boxes sprouted at the shop like weeds. Emptied of their treasures, we stored them in every available space to

126

await another use. I found one large enough to enable the kitten to move around but small enough, I hoped, to make him feel safe. We cut air holes in his new home for convalescing kittens and secured the top. As I gentled him next to the wood-stove, I heard a faint rustle like unseen sprites, jostling, settling to sleep. Leaning over, I felt a breath against my cheek, smelling of roses and sandalwood; his resting place, the box, had traveled from France, carrying soothing balms for the weary travelers to our gardens. Fitting, I thought.

The next morning I shuffled to the back door in my pre-coffee haze. Hearing me, Ingrid startled awake and followed to check on our patient.

"Wait a minute." I detoured to the percolator and poured a cup of courage. I bent close to the box. Silence and stillness absolute. I reached to remove the lid. A blur of black and white, gray and furry fury jack-in-the boxed from the carton, sprang to the top of the stove, scrambled across to a chair and streaked under the curtained sink to hide beneath a shelf of Comet and Dawn and Clorox in the furthest, darkest corner.

Ingrid spent the rest of the morning, first on her haunches then flat on her stomach, holding out a saucer of milk, her hand disappearing into the dark recesses beyond the curtain. About three that afternoon, she called me to join her on the floor. From under the sink, we heard a timid spit and then a tiny hiss and, at last, the sound of a hungry kitten lapping milk.

We named him Spencer for his dignified manner. Keeping his distance from humanity, he preferred to choose his own time and place for a little companionship. He spent some afternoons observing Kim on the days she helped Mom pot up roses. On rare occasions, I was graced with his contemplative presence while I weeded out a border. But he retained his wariness, finally taking up residence in the barn with Josie, our Great Pyrenees, becoming her second-in-command as guardian for our herd of Angora goats. He grew to the size and stature of a half-pint lion cub, possessing great dignity behind his large startled eyes.

He lived to a grand old age up on his hill, a distant but treasured member of our family. The only time we ever saw him let down his guard was late at night when he'd settle to sleep tucked up against Josie's soft white belly.

Highest Form of Flattery

The picture, depicting a cuffed bracelet carved with roses, took up not much more than a column inch among Victoria magazine's "Favorite Things," the details another inch - jewelry cast from marble dust, spangled with daisies, irises, roses. At the end of the ad, the Canadian address and telephone number I carried around in my head for a while, referring back to the picture every few days. The pendulum of indecision swinging among my choices - buy a lot, buy one, give it up, go out to the garden. Finally I called Canada and talked to Helen, artisan and small business owner herself. Reassuring me with tales of her own daily agonies in the world of commerce, she commended my jewelry choices, ending the call with a cheerful "Have a good day, eh."

It proved to be a good decision. I placed another order at the end of the month, another four weeks later. Reba, shop owner from across the mountain in the thriving heart of tourist Mecca, Maggie Valley, stuck her head in the door. "Hellooo!" That time again. Lifting a teapot in shades of amber and shaped like a cabbage, she checked the maker. Using a little sleight of mouth to distract me, a running monologue about her busy summer and her wealth of sales, she sniffed a candle, looking for the box holding its companions, noted the brand, and slid it to the back of the shelf.

She circled right, obeying the merchant's writ of customer habits. My jewelry display, covering a table top three feet by four feet, with a little extra boost in retail space provided by a stack of my best leather-bound books, was next on the inventory pilfering circuit.

I could tell when she spotted them, my marble dust beauties. She froze, caught herself, then began berating her local merchant's association for its refusal to "grow with the times." She glanced up. I looked away. Positioning herself between me and the table, she picked up the box of a pair of iris-shaped earrings, tilted it. Nothing – no address, no name, just a small white brocade box. I made a note to call Helen and thank her.

It proved too much for Reba. She turned, looked up, waving the earrings. "Where did you get these?" Seeing my smile, she added, "These would be lovely in my shop."

"Yes, they would. They're lovely in mine."

"Well, can I have the contact information? It's not like we're competitors." She waved her hand in the direction of Asheville. I assumed she intended to flit her fingers in the direction of her own renowned shopper's paradise.

"No. Sorry."

For many years, we were the only shop in our area to sell Helen's beautiful jewelry. Reba continued to visit, purloining any vendors she could, but I outlasted her. She sold her shop, retired and moved to Florida. The next owner introduced herself over a cup of tea out on the porch. Over the next leisurely hour, we talked of our struggles and our doubts about success with our chosen dreams. She bought an English rose, 'Sweet Juliet,' to plant outside her newly christened shop, "Blessings," and gave me her card with "10% off" scribbled on the back. She left with a brochure for The Herb of Grace and a contact number for the maker of a line of beautiful marble jewelry.

The Benefits of Ownership

In the land of dirt and flowers where the customary attire rotates between overalls in winter and a baggy pair of shorts for summer, she looked out of place, with her pressed, black dress pants and white, silk shirt under a tailored black blazer, as if she'd lost her way to a political convention or a committee meeting.

I smiled, said, "Hello." Stiffening, she sniffed as if I'd stepped over some line of familiarity. Thoroughly chastised, I returned to the couple – very much at home – holding a 14-inch Guy Wolfe creation, its rim fluted, terracotta washed pale.

On the counter, the two had assembled their own little garden – 'Pink Chintz' thyme, a Lavender 'Provence,' a Rosemary 'Tuscan Blue,' a 'Berggarten' sage, pineapple sage, and a chocolate mint.

"We want a container herb garden. What do you think?" They waggled the pot.

"Uh, well." Behind them, I could see the woman, still in high dudgeon over my unintended faux pas, whatever that might have been. Lifting first a silver tea caddy, then a porcelain spoon rest, she set each down again as if she were appraising the inventory and finding it wanting.

I looked back at the couple still clutching their Guy Wolfe pot, wistful smiles dimpling their cheeks.

"The thyme and the lavender, and the rosemary are all native to a Mediterranean climate, so they need a soil that's free draining, and they like baking under a hot sun. But the sage likes it not quite so dry and hot and the mint's just a bully. It needs a pot of its own. And three plants in a container this size, maybe, for a little while," I said.

They looked like I'd stolen their grape Popsicles, holding them just out of reach under that Tuscan sun I'd talked about. As they absorbed the injustice of such opinionated plants, behind them, finishing her critique of the main shop room, the black-suited woman walked into the hallway. With a finger, she nudged a mirror, leveled it to her satisfaction and moved on to see what the trio of Parisian café scenes was getting up to.

"Let me show you a couple of troughs I have. Might be more suitable." I set the Guy Wolfe pot down on the counter and steered the herb folks toward the door.

I called down the hall to the woman critiquing the inventory, my eyes shifting from the book room to the closed kitchen door, the privacy sign a study in bold red and white.

"I'll be right back."

"Don't you have anything approaching a true antique bowl in this place?" She looked down from her very great height upon my lowly head.

"Yellow Wear? Banded? Even, Dear God, an unglazed?"

We're tough, we women of the soil. Long-suffering. For a time. I retreated.

Back outside, I showed my herb gardeners the hypertufa troughs displayed along the pathway in front of the porch.

"They look kind of unfinished, don't they – sort of like concrete dish pans. What's down there?"

Underneath the old maple sat a few of our larger pots. Pointing to a cobalt urn two feet across, I said, "This would be about right for the lavender and rosemary, the thyme. Plant them in a mix of about 70/30, potting soil to oyster shell or perlite. The sages'll do okay in straight potting soil, and the mints will gallivant all over the place on their own in just about any kind of dirt."

They shook their heads. They had fallen in love with the Guy Wolfe and nothing else would do. I sold it to them. They bought the herbs, all of them. Holding my tongue, saying a prayer on behalf of the innocent, I helped them load.

Peggy, my cranberry tea and fig soap regular, was standing at the counter when I came back inside. From somewhere in the back, I heard a clunk, followed by a thud.

"Peggy, let me get you a cup of tea before you go," I said before darting down the hall.

Inside the shop during hot days, the songs of Thrushes and Cardinals silenced, and the windows closed against the heat, music – quiet, lovely music – played in the background for my customers and for me. Pacabell's concerto covered the sound of my footsteps, the easing open of the privacy door. I stood there next to the "Private - No Entrance" sign, looking at the spreading posterior of the woman rummaging through my cabinets. On my worktable, she'd assembled all my personal pottery. Reaching around the corner, I flipped the CD player to off. She whirled, recovered as only someone with the proverbial brass balls can, and lifted an earthenware bowl over a hundred years old from my table. John had bought it for me for our second anniversary.

"I'll take this. These, too, if the price is right."

"These too" had lived with me for years, since my mother and I found them on a shopping trip in the haunts of a coastal town back home. I couldn't afford them both, so Mom bought one of them for me, just because.

Sometimes, there isn't enough money in the world, and sometimes it can be a mighty fine thing to own the place. I saw her out.

The Last Straw

Late arrivals, especially on Sundays, were welcomed with a smile, always, sinking heart and tattered hospitality notwithstanding. And, now, the ass-end of a Suburban pretty much blocked the private entrance gate to the nursery, a swarm emerging from the vehicle looking like locusts on the last day of harvest. When they were forced to funnel down to cross the bridge, we realized the swarm that had us paralyzed at the window, actually numbered only four. The sun straddling the ridgeline cast long shadows, tracing the trees in gold and copper and ripe melon; the breeze laden with the smell of burnt sugar, our katsura tree shaking free its autumn leaves. The earth shouting its glory was lost in the clamoring cacophony that seemed to surround the approaching family like a fog.

They never stopped talking.

What kinda place is this?" He was maybe fourteen a little boy trying on a lout's body. "Oh, cool." He'd spotted the goats and was lumbering straight up on a collision course with the electric fence. John moved to head him off.

The dad plowed to the next goal, strapped sandals slapping the grass into shape, scattering golden leaves in his wake. "Ok, let's see what there is to see."

The mom, long denim skirt scraping her shoe tops, turned, clutched my shoulder and shouted, "Cilantro, do you have cilantro?"

"Only in spring." My words caught in the whirlwind as she spun, hustling to catch up to her husband.

"Roger! I want to see if they have cilantro! Remember that recipe on the Food Channel! Roger, wait up!" She tackled him at the steps.

Carried along in her force field, I followed. Up on the mountain, kicking up a tapestry of fallen needles and leaves, John herded the rampaging adolescent.

Forgotten, especially by Mom and Dad, a younger boy ran screaming across the bridge. "Mom, Mom, Mom, Mom! You better wait for me. I mean it. You better wait!" Behind the house, Duffy howled a tenor to the child's tragic aria, but his mother, still lamenting the absence of cilantro, remained impervious to the boy's demands.

"Roger! Here's rosemary. I've heard of rosemary. It was on the Food Channel, right?"

In a world to himself, devoid of wives and food channels, Roger rapped his knuckles against one of the porch pillars, "Pine? I bet it's pine. Yep! Gotta be pine. I know my wood."

From the arbor, the smaller boy stood transfixed, his mouth hanging open in disbelief. He was being ignored. Suddenly screeching at the injustice of his recalcitrant mother, the youngster sprinted across the garden headlong into his mother. Alas, to no avail. Looking past him, over him, through him, she glared, instead, in the direction of her eldest. He was halfway down the hillside, returning from his thwarted battle among the goats, kicking the berries off a clump of *Callicarpa*. Bracing herself, she bellowed. "Michael! Get down here! Right now! Remember your punishment! Take care of Joseph!"

Silenced, Joseph watched his mother walk away.

Overhead, in a sky worthy of paradise, a Redtail Hawk soared upon the winds of autumn. His cry, too, falling in the forest alone, remained unheard. Back at the bench of culinary herbs, Mom picked up a pot of lemon thyme. "Roger." She followed him into the shop. "Thyme. Thyme was on the Food Channel."

Stepping inside the shop, Roger stopped. The wife stumbled into him. He whistled, "You could use some more room in here. Can't swing a cat."

At that, I saw John slink down the hall and into the kitchen, abandoning ship. I looked at the clock. Twenty minutes till closing time. I passed one of our herb charts over to, what was her name?

"Hi, I'm Bobbie. May I help you?" I found myself addressing the back of her head.

"Roger, here's what we need." She jabbed a finger at the chart.

The minutes slugged by like molasses until our clocks chimed five o'clock.

"I'm sorry. It's closing time."

138

They lingered on until five after, then ten after. I started turning off the lights. With a huff, they departed herbless, collecting Michael along the way, as he prepared to roll Joseph down the hill inside one of our French urns aiming for a Japanese maple. I watched as Roger and wife, still talking, headed toward their car, the boys waiting at the bridge, taking random kicks at each other's shins. Relief washed over me like a tide of the chilled sauvignon blanc waiting in the fridge.

John sat slumped in his chair. I joined him across the table, shut my eyes bonding with the silence. Five minutes later, they were back, pounding at the door.

Roger was peering through the top of the door, his nose smudging the glass, the wife behind him. "Hey! Hey! We locked our keys in the car."

I turned the lock, twisted the knob, and with surprising agility, dodged a very pissed off door. Behind me, John, revived, once again had my back.

Subdued by finding themselves in the land of wild beasties with a dark and spooky night coming on, son younger and son elder huddled together at the bottom of the porch steps. Inside, their parents battled their own bumps in the night, hovering over the phone, pleading for rescue. The motor club relented.

"One hour." They looked at each other in dismay.

We knew better. No one made it to this valley from an unfamiliar elsewhere in the dark in a mere hour. They were pitiful. We took pity. But shame on me, my Southern manners ended at our kitchen door. I seated them in the shop library, called the boys, set up trays. I filled the kettle while John made coffee. I sliced the leftover Italian loaf, the only bread in our near-empty cupboards, and made ham sandwiches. I took the last half round of Gouda from the refrigerator, cut it into wedges, arranged the last of my stash of succulent green grapes on a plate, stuck a couple of bananas alongside. John and I carried the offering to the library, along with a plate of the day's remaining teacakes. I knew better than to expect a smile or a thank you, but a whine?

"What's that? That's not bread. I won't eat it." Joseph said, then threatened. "I'll puke."

Taking note of him for the first time since they arrived, his mother looked at him, then leaned over and cooed. "That's all right, Joey, she'll make you another sandwich."

"With real bread." He sniffled.

"Sorry, I'm out of white bread. This home-baked, three hours in the making bread, is it," I said.

His mother held his face, adoringly, between her hands and pleaded. "How about a bowl of cereal. You'll like that, Joey?" She looked at me, raised her eyebrows. "You do have cereal, don't you?"

Two bowls of John's Cheerios and three hours later, salvation arrived in a AAA motor club service truck.

We started clearing the site for the new shop a few days later.

Act Two

Starting Anew

Waiting had been hard. Every winter, as we closed the doors on another season, we hoped next year, next spring, we'd be able to start building the new shop. I knew from the beginning where it needed to be. I said as much to John when we passed it the first time. Before we bought the farm. Before I was readying my arguments against the little white house on its little hump by the side of the road. Passing, I turned my head and fell in love with a ruin – an old springhouse open to the sky – tiny courtyard cloistered in stone, a rock wall, rock steps leading up from the road; and an ancient hemlock standing sentinel, boughs bowing, sweeping low as if it were growing in holy ground. Behind, poplar trees with trunks so massive they groaned, marched to the ridge top.

"It's perfect," I said.

But our new farm ended just outside the spring-fed gates to paradise. The courthouse records revealed an absentee owner from Florida and an address. I wrote, told them we were interested, and if ever they decided to sell?

Three years passed until one June Monday found me picking blueberries – one for the bowl, one luscious berry for me. Straightening, stretching, I threw back my head, inhaling an elixir of spices and herbs and clean, clear water and caught sight of a vagabond band of gypsies heading my way. Back in this world, a very ordinary, albeit attractive, family of four, ambled down the road coming from the rubble of the five-acre parcel and the minivan parked alongside.

Her smile, like the day, appeared full of hope. "Hi, my name's Annie Taylor." Pointing back toward the stone wall, the magic tree, and my dreams, she said, "I got your letter."

Strange that we'd never heard her story – the story of the five-acre parcel and an old gabled farmhouse. Annie and her first husband fell in love with the house and dreamed of their kids around a country table. Two days and a night after they'd brought the last load over the mountain, carried the boxes of toys inside, set them down in the front room, the house burned. To the ground, leaving them with only ashes. Everybody made it out, but the loss and the elbowed whispers about "funny business," cost Annie her marriage and her liking of old houses.

She wanted to sell. We wanted to buy.

And so on that afternoon, once all papers were signed and legalities sorted, we took possession of a dream, or at least the bare bones of one. After dinner that evening, I walked over, stood under the hemlock. A hundred years back, a farmer and his folks felled a congregation of poplar trees and hemlocks and sweet dogwoods from the lower fifty or so feet of a hillside so steep they had to lash themselves to the upper trees to make their first cuts. Then like slicing through a Christmas fruitcake, they gouged a wedge out of the bank, leaving skittering rocks and dangling roots. They smoothed and leveled the rough site and built a sturdy house for a family. Until fire left only charred beams and crumbling stone.

Above the conflagration, in the shade of the remaining old growth poplars and oaks, wild *Hydrangeas* sprouted and trillium and ginseng and the bells of Solomon's seal grew and blossomed. Grace notes of maidenhair fern settled in pockets of soil between the rocks. And a single species primrose provided a flame of gold. This would be a hidden garden just large enough for a lone contemplative in search of solitude at the end of a busy day in a happy little shop.

I walked back, the sun dipping behind the ridge, a light in the kitchen welcoming me.

143

The actual building unfolded like a family reunion – prolonged over many months and many miles. It started with a brother, six hundred miles south.

To call Barry anything other than a brother would be misleading, although he is, in truth, my sister's husband. Still, he's family – call in the middle of the night family; think nothing of driving a hundred miles to make sure you've turned off the water family. And even though by profession he's an architect of sacred spaces, he'll design a small shop and make it wondrous, and he'll refuse to take money for it, because he's family. And that's why, even after all these years, I still feel guilty.

The footprint of the old farmhouse dictated the size – 36 feet long and 24 feet wide. Outside, I wanted a wide verandah, 12 feet deep, running the length of the building, so that those breaking bread and drinking tea would now have a place to gather out of the elements. Stepping down, rounding the corner, gardeners would enter the tiny courtyard with its rough stone walls and pass through the door into the springhouse, still absent its roof.

Inside, I needed a restroom and a kitchen, a counter, and open space. Outside, I wanted the roof pitched steep like a fairy-tale, its walls stuccoed, a skill, an art practiced for over a thousand years and still practiced by my father. Barry took my scribblings, suitable for a refrigerator magnet, and my air-fairy instructions and turned them into my dream made tangible. Like works of art, his preliminary drawings and blueprints graced our walls.

144

Meanwhile, down the road, a stroke of good luck was about to fall. Our neighbors were calculating the board feet in 20 poplar trees, tall and straight, and a single white oak, ancient and massive, felled by the rural electric co-op during its spring clearing campaign.

Carl and May farmed across the road and three curves down on land that had been in May's family for five generations. They were the second neighbors we met, after Millie. A couple of hundred yards from their double-wide, their only child, Pearl, lived in hers – her children dividing their time between Pearl's house and Papaw's and Mamaw's. Above, on a site designed by a Divine architect, the original farmhouse stood empty. "Too cold to live in, and the floors are a chore to sweep." But May couldn't bear to see it pulled down. "And it's so pretty setting up there, under them oaks."

White-faced Herefords grazed the ridges behind their house, the small flat fields between laid-to tobacco. After harvest, you could see the progression of greening from the burley sticks as you passed on your way to the store in the spring of the year, fertilizing fields for the next growing year.

But at the fourth bend in the road, trees, grown tall, threatened the electric lines and now, like fallen giants, lay beside the road. We made Carl and May an offer for the trees and paid to have them sawn by another neighbor with a portable sawmill. Unlike lumber purchased from a home improvement store – hauled a thousand miles across country – our two-by-fours measured a full 2 inches by 4 inches instead of the 1 3/8 x 3 3/8 inches off the rack. Two-by-sixes, four-byeights and timbers hewn to beams a foot-square were stacked and waiting.

The weather held, fine and cool, as John and James wrestled the first load onto Carl's hay trailer. The 8-N chugged down the hill and back up a total of five times. The morning of the sixth day dawned with a taint of sulfur in the air. A weather breeder. As John headed down to Carl's, the wind began its howl down the Eastern slope, the clouds above his head skidding to the east, a sure sign of an impending torrent.

He knew better. Enough board feet remained for two, maybe three more trips to the barn, but there was that storm a comin'. Friends and neighbors, Brass and Lenny came down to help. They stacked lumber three feet high, then started shoving boards into cracks, until the last of the board feet sat on the trailer awaiting the final voyage to the barn. Brass cranked the hitch down, slapped Lenny on the back and circled a hand above his head. John shoved the 8-N into first gear and chugged toward home.

It took a minute or two for John to realize the horizon over the tractor's nose was sinking and the hood was rising toward the tops of the hemlocks. Later, he told me that as he hung onto the steering wheel, his knees gripping the seat, his life didn't so much pass before his mind's eye, as did the thought that this was a mighty small valley with an acerbic penchant for a good story. Nightfall would find it a topic of conversation at every table down at the café.

I caught sight of the Clampett-styled caravan from the potting shed, an open-mouthed customer at my side. We

146

watched as Carl's powerful John Deere rounded the bend, the 8-N attached with an umbilical cord of chain, its nose striking asphalt every few feet, dragging a hillbilly load of wood on a flat tired trailer. Shoulders hunched, caps pulled low against the rain, the crew looked plum pitiful.

The wood was laid to dry inside the barn. For the next month, to walk into the barn was to see it rain from the rafters. We figured a year's drying time would be about right. It took three.

At last, after a summer of blessed events – the arrival of nephew Stephen and niece Ingrid to lend a hand – and far too many aggravations, we broke ground.

The winter before had dumped four feet of snow on the creek in a twenty-four-hour period, stranding John on the other side of the mountain and penalizing Kim and me to round-the-clock servitude, sweeping snow off hoop-houses, greenhouses, hemlocks, spruces, sculpted maples.

Once the snow melted, we became bog creatures, slogging through mud to the barn, returning in layers so thick our heads struck the door jambs on our way in to thaw up for the next round of chores.

Then, the weather gods sneered in mirthless chuckles and drought descended.

On day one of the summer building project, John set out armed with a pickaxe. Ingrid joined him after a breakfast smoothie. She found him sitting on a rock contemplating a series of small divots pocked in the ground, the foundation strings trembling at his labors.

"They look like the efforts of a bunch of fledglings in a preschool for woodpeckers." He kicked at the ground. It was too dry even for dust.

John still refuses to talk about the jackhammer. He rented a backhoe. Over the next four weekends, Ingrid reported to the worksite to help John dig the foundation. She held string-line, peered through the transit and did an admirable job of step and fetch it

Ingrid left us, returning north to her home in Canada, a poignant goodbye, surrendering her slot in the workforce.

It was time to pour the foundation, the footers. John had squirreled away vacation time, not to be squandered this early in construction, and the most I could spare at any one time was the shop's weekly two days of recovery. Not to worry, we told Millie and for insurance dropped the word down at the cafe that we'd like to hire a couple of able-bodied neighbors for a few days, paying top dollar. Silence fell. Quiet ensued. As if an alien abduction had coincided with the arrival of the concrete trucks, the valley emptied. Not only the able-bodied went missing, but their spouses as well. On our own, and pouring day loomed.

During lunch time in the cafeteria, over tuna fish and fries, John related this phenomenon to a table of his peers – engineers and techies, administrators and housekeepers. Getting up from the table, John shook his head to a chorus of commiseration. Kevin followed him out.

Besides the role of friend, Kevin also worked as a special processes engineer, but his Dad "operated heavy equipment in Long Island for the best part of forty years" and could turn his hand to most anything. Up until that point, all John knew of Kevin's Dad was that he'd seen his first ever cow in a South Carolina field on his way from Long Island to retirement next street over from his son. And apparently, son Kevin, by childhood osmosis, had absorbed a few of his dad's building skills. They owned wheelbarrows and could travel the two plus hours - one way - the next week to see to it. John stopped short of a hug and settled for a grateful handshake.

The sun was just polishing the tops of the trees when Kevin and his dad, Bob, slammed the doors of their Chevy stepside - construction loaded – and reached for the thermos I held ready in my hands. Along with strong, hot coffee, I also hefted my trusty trowel, badge of the day's "master leveler to grader."

We joined forces, stood at the ready. Two trucks, only half-loaded in order to scale the mountain, were due any minute.

Concrete truck number one arrived. The driver explained it was his first day on the job. When he took out a small tree, the drive informed us, "I don't think I can do this. It's my first day." The truck idled while concrete continued to rotate to solidity.

Concrete truck number two pulled up. His cap riding low over furrowed brow, the driver spat out the window, bulls-eyeing a dandelion. Climbing down from his rig, he sauntered over to the first truck, flicked his head and said, "Get out."

We relaxed. Experience guided first one truck, then the other into place.

Meanwhile, trowel at the ready, I began slicing, mashing, smearing concrete, trying to manipulate it into, more or less, a level plane, before it morphed into a Serengeti of archeological shards. The muscles in my upper arm knotted like tree roots, and all I hoped for was an end to my misery.

We adopted Kevin and Dad Bob as esteemed family members.

The next week, another stellar friend in need, Buck, took over trowel duty to help John lay block. Freed, I hustled back to the potting shed, delighted to wrangle seventy-pound bags of soil instead.

Kim stood inside one square, floor joists striking her midsection, and wove fiberglass insulation between the hangers. From another square, I bent, tugged, and did my own weaving. John, meanwhile, shoved 4' x 8' sheets of 3/4" tongue and groove plywood into place and nailed them down. We labored engulfed in air so hot it silenced the cicadas, and so thick it flowed down our faces like treacle. I swiped at a stray hair, transferring the sweat of tedium from arm to brow. Another tickle, a tangle along my forehead, another swipe. A breeze, playing hide and seek. Another thwack from the staple gun, another blow from the hammer. High above, the breeze, joining its playmates, turned bully, darkening the clouds, raising the hair along the back of my neck.

It became a race now. Hunkering down, we bent, we pulled, we stapled, we hammered – four bays left, now three. My concentration narrowed to a four-foot square, muscle memory taking over.

Where sun, only moments before, had scorched even toughened skin, clouds black as pitch gathered, blocking out the light. The wind stilled. A hush enveloped us. Through my mind flicked Sunday school thoughts of the four horsemen of the apocalypse. Kim looked toward the horizon. "Holy crap!"

Then, we heard it – the roar of a thousand beasts, the lashing of a thousand trees, rain beating the earth into rivers of mud. As John pounded the last nail, as Kim and I drug tarps over the finished floor, tossed rocks up to anchor them from the wind, all hail broke loose. Huddled at the door to the springhouse, we looked like drowned rats, Dickens' street urchins peering out at the aftermath. The storm had softened to a gentle rain, drowning the villainous drought in a sea of muck.

We could have used a little divination, a few castings of the bones. "Weather" was upon us.

A fleeting fall issued in a winter swollen with snow. John's brothers blew in on the worst blizzard of the year. Ed and Dave, along with nephew Eddie, drove in on a Friday. Eddie's brother, Eric, rode north and arrived Saturday morning as the wind chill plunged to minus 20. Kim's Sam showed up disguised as the Pillsbury Doughboy in sub-zero Carhartts. Adversity sparked the lifeblood and a challenge added the spice. I heard laughter cloaked in bravado and cuss words.

Driven to distraction by the blizzard winds, snow clung against sidewalls and coated rafters, frosted beards and stocking caps. On an egg hunt for two by six framing timbers, Eric unearthed a missing toolbox, a pyramid of twenty-penny nails and an empty thermos before spooking an avalanche to reveal a stack of the required poplar boards. I handed John a full thermos and took the snow-crusted one back across the horseshoe parking lot, down the springhouse steps, through the garden door into a costume party all in white. Blueberry bushes dressed as hags in ermine. Boxwoods shrouded as monks in a hump-shouldered march. Rose canes bent beneath glittering dragon scales. The wind shrieked ahead of me, denuding Japanese maples, stripping *Clematis*. Every-one stood around in tatters, shivering, the party over.

For five days everybody worked non-stop for hours on end. A miser's respites consisted of coffee and grilled sandwiches, soggy and cold from the trek across the garden. The wind dying down teased us with expectations of thawing necks and fingers, only to rage triumphant once again. Snow had to be shoveled away from the door, swept off stairs, cleared from the floor, constantly. Kim and I tangoed as toadies, coffee haulers, and unskilled labor.

"Brace that board. Put your shoulder into it! Come on woman!" I think they enjoyed "the help" far too much.

When the string of utility lights could no longer penetrate the dark and the cold numbed grips around hammer and nail, the brothers and nephews (at times accompanied by John) would drive up the mountain to Sally's cabins and warm up with a wood fire and a bottle of good Kentucky Bourbon. I would creak back to the house, open the back door, and collapse, letting the banked wood fire soothe my aching body. Kim would hug me goodbye and head home with Sam in tow, unless she too just needed somewhere to crash her weary bones.

On the last day, but one, the snow clouds began to thin – torn tatters across a pale sky – and evening glowed in the light of a descending sun. By noon the following day, jackets were shed. By two, sleeves rolled up. By end of day, we stood looking to the heavens where walls rose tall and rafters opened to the sky. With the help of three brothers and two sons, and a daughter and a friend, a thing most corporal had been created from the seeds of hope. Ed owned a printing company. He sat at the same desk where his father once worked, and his father before him. Dave worked there as well – marketing, as did Eddie, learning the business. Eric traveled for a major manufacturer. And John, with his degree in philosophy, managed the IT department for the company that produced the Abrams tank engine. Sam, Kim's best buddy? Well, he was a carpenter, formerly a teacher. These were their day jobs. Off hours, they built cathedrals.

Those rafters opening to the elements needed a roof, and it ended up being, not by design, a one-man job. The Philosopher retrieved his tin snips and a very long ladder. "Grueling" is the way John remembers it. But the actual work went well, without incident – until an early morning of heavy dew and a temperature of 32 degrees. Busy in the potting shed, I only heard about it when I looked up to see John at the door, white-faced.

As he told it, "I was on the back side at the peak, nail in one hand, hammer in the other, when I started to slide. Shot right off the roof, did a one-eighty and landed on the bank in a mess of ferns and little yellow flowers."

We had another gathering of family, this time during a week of clear, cool days in early April. We all, I think, tend to paint special memories with a wash of gold, tinted in blush and pearl and opal – the colors of the buds on the roses swelling in the garden. It's the richness I remember most about those days – when many of my folks came to help.

The reality, though, is that metal lath, the material upon which stucco adheres, is evil and John's hands bled for days as he tried to hold and nail it to the outer walls. Hours would pass before I realized all I'd heard from him were some descriptive cuss words. And, no matter how fit a young woman may be, bags of stucco mix are heavy when you're trying to lift them three feet off the ground into a cement mixer. When nephew Stephen arrived to play co-mud boy, it spurred a little competition resulting in a dropped. It exploded in a zephyr of cement dusting them both a spectral haint gray. Grit up their noses and in their ears tended to settle things down a bit.

I signed on as apprentice to my father, the master. To see him trowel stucco on the vertical was to watch a dance of artistry. Each pass practiced over a career spanning all the decades of my life. Not a smear of fat oiled the sinews on my dad's 5'6", 130-pound frame as he bent, dipped, scooped and scraped mud onto the trowel. Stretching upright, turning, he smoothed the heavy wet stucco onto the lathed wall, spilling not a dollop. His apprentice, meanwhile, squatted, then dumped and pushed mud onto her trowel. Reaching slapping and clumping mud onto the wall, I dropped at least a third of my load with each pass. But I have to say, I may have looked like a clodhopper instead of a danseur noble, and we could have sculpted a small David with the cement I dropped, but the wall I finished proved I was my father's child. It was beautiful. My father remained a hundred paces (at least) ahead of me.

There are some levels of tired that are so weary they defy words. The first day of stucco finished on a note of such fatigue it carried its own kind of delusion. Twilight, at the end of the first day, found me prone on the kitchen floor. I opened one eye to see Kim emerge in a cloud of steam from the bathroom, toweling her hair. His hair still peaking from his own shower, Stephen leaned against the door. I closed my eyes.

Kim said, "We're meeting Sam in Asheville for a little bluegrass, maybe a little jazz, a little jitterbugging."

I think I heard her cut a little bounce-step as the door closed on all that youth. I rolled over and watched John, slumped against the wall applying bandages to his fingers. After a day of cooking, toting, serving, cleaning and general dogs bodying, Mom, Carla and her young ones, our Maisie and Molly, sat around the kitchen table murmuring stories into the evening air. Dad joined them. At least he had the grace to slurp his third cup of coffee quietly.

Dusk on the final day of stucco found my dad and me up on ladders plastering, smoothing the last coat in the last corner. Below, John scrounged around on the ground – a churned-up concoction of clay, rock, and charcoaled wood – looking for errant pieces of metal, bent nails, the detritus remaining as testament of great labor.

"Hey, looky here," he yelled.

I hobbled down the ladder, walked over to where he was eyeing a tangle of green. As he lifted his foot, I could see discs the color of seashells floating atop the green, translucent in the fading light. I dropped to my knees, leaned over, and buried my nose in the blossoms. Inhaled. It smelled like my grandmother's garden on summer mornings, the year my little sister was born. They were petunias, the old fragrant variety. The seed, exposed after how many years, had sent roots deep into the soil and flowered again as a benediction on family, on love, on honest labor.

Although Dad would live his allotted years, and then some, this was his grand finale – his last job on the scaffolding. After, every time I walked in the door, I'd lay my hand against the swirls of stucco and bow my head at the blessing.

The scaffolding moved inside. Friends arrived to swing a hammer. From up holler, Fred, like a capuchin monkey, scaled a ladder, his weight in plasterboard resting on top of his head. Jack and his dad drove two hours to lift, carry, lend a shoulder, tape a seam, nail a board, then drove two hours back home. I resurrected my trowel and plastered walls. John and Sam fashioned shelving from fluted roofing metal stood on end and woven with hand planed poplar boards.

Over the mountain inside the cavity of Sam's shop, twelve-foot doors crafted of a double thickness of Appalachian oak nailed together with square-head cut nails, spanned an eight-foot width atop saw horses. We – John, Kim, and myself – stood looking down at the smooth, buttery texture of old-growth oak. Already, two sets of cafe doors stood against the wall.

"Sam, they're beautiful, like an invitation to enchantment," I said.

Kim laughed and then looked at me. She felt it too.

Opening day loomed large. John would arrive home from his hour and a half commute, grab a little dinner, spend a couple of hours hanging windows or running a water line. Kim drove over every morning for toast and coffee. Heading for the shop with our second cups, we'd set to on the day's agenda – trimming between walls and ceiling with cream-colored braided rope instead of wood because we'd run low on funds, painting the plywood floor lavender because the budget didn't spread to wood or tile, cleaning until our knuckles bled.

Sunset on a late April day, the big brown truck wove through the valley delivering goods to the community, and this time we waved Joshua up the hill to the New Shop. Christmas in spring, we tore open boxes of teas, soaps, jewelry, garden art – fresh inventory for our new beginnings. As I headed to the greenhouses to start pulling flats of perennials and herbs, and pots of roses and heathers, and *Clematis* and *Camellias* for the newly erected plant tables, Kim obsessed into a styling frenzy. She pulled her first all-nighter since college, sleeping on an old loveseat we'd positioned in the alcove where new gardening books slept around her.

Two days later, those doors swung wide. "Welcome!"

Build a Shop and They Will Come . . .
Eventually

In my memory, the sun was shining and the sweet green earth emitted the fragrance of a thousand violets and a thousand hyacinths. Rain from the night before pooled in the leaves of Lady's Mantle, frilling the ground around the tall planters made from flue liners and painted the color of lilacs. Stooping at the garden gate, Ruby, an impasto painting in jeans and t-shirt, spread mulch between mounds of 'Pere David' Corydalis. Kim and I waited on the Verandah.

I'd managed to get the dirt from under my fingernails, and Kim looked quite elegant in spite of her late night with the packing boxes and the early morning tweak of her displays. A lifetime's collection of damask, linen, French cottons, and centerpieces blooming with apple blossoms and early roses transformed our motley crew of tables – Eliza Doolittles into Fair Ladies. Even my old farm table, drug from my old Pickens barn and hauled around from pillar to post, looked fetching in a faded blue toile. Like a reunion of distant friends, the chairs gathered around the tables showing off their different pedigrees – iron garden, folding cafe, white wicker, bentwood. In the shop's small kitchen (at this sight, I pinched myself), the kettle steamed and I could smell the sweet, yeasty scones fresh from the oven.

Outside, the gravel had been raked, every weed pulled. Potted foxgloves graced the small walled courtyard, their strawberries and cream blooms nodding in a gentle breeze. Within the crumbling springhouse, fragrant with the ghosts of fresh butter, fresh cream, and a breath of rum-soaked watermelon for a hot summer's day, resided a gardener's treasures – vintage watering cans, Victorian border tiles, flaked white birdbaths – all whispering "Take me home."

On either side of the shop, benches sagged with the weight of so much horticultural beauty. Groomed to perfection, the perennials and roses, like beauty queens, strutted their wire-mesh runways. Even their grass green pots shined.

Inside my head, a bell tolled. Opening time, a new season, a new era. And the world around us stood empty of all humanity. The roads, the parking lot, even the fields looked like the Resurrection had come and gone, only we three failing to make the cut. No birds sung from the trees. No bunnies snuggled in the underbrush. No squirrels thieved sunflower seeds.

We were alone, and I began to panic, hearing my abiding scold, "Well, who did you think you are anyway?"

The sun shining its blessings on the day turned into a glaring spotlight upon all my warts and failures. Behind us, a spell had been cast, our beautiful shop, our wondrous plants victims of my hubris. The minutes ticked by.

Kim and I spotted them at the same time – four cars, creeping down the mountain, shepherded by our over-the-hill neighbor, revving at fifteen miles an hour on the way to his breakfast at the cafe – and we exhaled in unison. We breathed again as two gracious ladies seated on the Verandah bit into their lemon and lavender scones and pronounced them "Better than Claridges!" And relaxed at last as guests, one after another, walked into the shop and said "Ooh..."

Thus, the morning and the afternoon of the first day passed. And at the sixth hour, we rested and saw that it had been good, very good.

In the Garden

A Blessed Rose and a Thorn in the Flesh

And now to introduce Ruby, out there spreading mulch.

Our customary Friday night found the eight of us, friends, ex-pats and escapees from the real world, down at the café. It looked like the whole community had turned out to celebrate the first few hours of a February thaw by ordering "Fresh Trout and Hushpuppies" or "Pasta Florentine," the specials of the day. Back in town from her winter hiatus in Miami - "What the hell possessed me" - Madeline was serving the fish to a couple from the Flats as we walked in the door and took our place in the queue. Lifting her "be with you in a minute" finger, she rolled her eyes as a new server tripped over the welcome mat, clutching a couple of plates in her white-knuckled fists.

The new "girl," Ruby according to her penciled nametag, stopped at the first booth, dropped the plates - pasta and a burger and fries - then spun back to the counter and grabbed an armful of menus. Jumbled together on the mat, we looked at her and she glared back until we got the message and meekly followed her to the big table in the back.

Resentment radiated from her curly brown hair to her size five shoes. Frown lines etched her eyes and age spots circled her tiny face. A couple of menus slid from her grasp onto the table, knocking over a saltshaker and relocating a basket of Waverlys. Her Bic high dived into a water glass. Jamming her fist into the glass, she retrieved the pen and shook it, spraying water droplets across three tables. She frowned at the glass – water now at low tide – and left it, a rebuke against needy diners everywhere.

One by one, she brought out our entrees, asked each time, "Whose is this?"

Most perplexing was the BLT, side of fries. Ruby held it over the table and waited, menacing a dare in our direction. John looked at me, I glanced at Liz, she peeked at Butch. Thus it continued, each passing the torch of noncommittal cowardice around the table. Arriving at the end where Lenny – left holding the metaphorical gauntlet – stuck his hand up. She shoved the plate under his nose and he, in line to inherit the earth, placed the sandwich alongside his Rainbow Trout special.

She got better. The next time we gathered, she had graduated to carrying two plates at a time, not always the right ones, but accepted by our craven lot anyway. But she looked on small talk as a frivolity and laughter as suspicious. When spoken to, she snapped one syllable replies. By mid-March, she'd honed her waitress skills to a dull edge, and we heard the occasional, unsolicited, "Damn."

Proving the theory that you can get used to even a burr under the saddle, the community tolerated her and over time developed a wary attachment. I think we all began to feel a grudging sort of respect, but we forever remained just a little afraid of Ruby – all 100 pounds of her.

Another spring spread through the valley, bringing with it renewal and a sense of anticipation. Outside, the first Cardinal of morning greeted the first light of day. I opened the door to the heated greenhouse where young tomato seedlings – 'Brandywine', 'Mr. Stripey,' and 'Mortgage Lifter', needed watering. In the next section over, 'Genovese' and 'Thai' basil, along with a trial of three new varieties, waited their turn, thirsty for a dose. On one of my interminable doubling backs to unkink the water hose, I noticed a little gray compact pull into the drive. I walked out to greet the driver. Long minutes passed while we studied each other. I had a feeling I knew what she wanted.

Rolling down the window, eyes narrowed to a suspicious slit, Ruby said, "Can I come to work here? They pay dirt down at the cafe." And, yes, I felt I must somehow be to blame.

Not an auspicious beginning, but I couldn't seem to come up with an excuse to say no, and she looked like she might growl or, worse, cry.

I said, "Yes."

I am eternally glad I didn't have time to think, to turn her away. Ruby became our rock, my guard dog in banty rooster disguise. Always arriving early to her post, she had the stamina of a marathoner and the strength of a stevedore, belying her look of fragility. She could wheel her barrow full of mulch up those hills as well as down. Don't tread on her borders; don't manhandle one of her *Geraniums*; and you'd best not malign a single member of The Herb of Grace family. She'd throw that 100 pounds at you like a sumo wrestler. But she could hear a slight in the most innocent of remarks. Took instruction as if it were criticism. Thorny as a multiflora rose. We all walked softly, every morning, creeping in her presence until we established what side of her bed she woke up on.

In time, I found out some of the answers to the whys of Ruby. More than four decades before her debut at the Creek Café, she'd married her one and only sweetheart on the eve of her high school graduation. Failing to infiltrate much of West Virginia, the sixties found girls still looking to Mrs. Cleaver for marital instruction – the little woman minded the hearth, scrubbed the clothes, cooked the dinner, and raised the children. Ruby never held a job outside the drudgery of housework and never asked questions of the man of the house. Then the tawdry little story unfolded once again – with an ugly underbelly. Hubby locked her out of his house, keeping all its contents, his new pick-up and his new girlfriend, leaving Ruby penniless (unless you counted the twelve-year-old Datsun) and very bitter.

"I hope the two of them rot in hell."

Through the years, when there was no money left over to pay the chief, I felt blessed to be able to pay her better than dirt.

A Hypertufa Folly of Hope

After a winter closed and bereft of customers and income; after dark months of spending, gambling on a future dependent upon fickle weather, fickle hope, fickle desire, every spring arrived, finding me frantic and ripe, not to say gullible, for any marketing opportunity.

Along with festivals, talks, singing, dancing, and dog-and-pony shows to ramp up business, we offered classes and the making of hypertufa garden features was a perennial favorite. A mixture of vermiculite, peat moss, and concrete, it mimicked the porous calcium carbonate stone used in the construction of English country house garden follies of the 17th and 18th centuries. We promoted our own folly by offering two classes each season. They filled quickly with a lot of grumbling from those put on a waiting list.

Gathered inside the old tobacco barn, this class of ten drenched souls squinted like baby owls into the gloom. The morning's sunshine had melted into a steady afternoon soaker. Lined up just inside the door stood buckets, hand trowels, rubber gloves, cans of cooking spray, assorted empty coffee cans, plastic pots, and the ingredients for our very own hypertufa creations. A water hose connected to the upper spring snaked across the barn floor.

Molds of choice for this class included three shoeboxes, a Tupperware cake-taker, and two trashcans. Standing next to their wives, a couple of husbands eyed each other's identical, purpose made, cardboard tubes fresh off the shelf of a local big-box store. One woman, dressed in perfectly creased jeans and tailored white blouse, drug in a wooden box big enough to house Josie our Great Pyrenees.

Eyeing one another, then the assembled paraphernalia atop the sawhorse table, they, finally, turned to me to take my measure. Like first graders suspicious of just what this so-called teacher was up to.

"Okay, let's get started." I clapped my hands, startling a dove off its rafter. To a pupil, the class flinched. I sighed.

"Mix one part of the Portland cement," I started.

"Part?" one of the women asked, her forehead creased, still wary.

"This." I lifted a coffee can. "Is a part. Now, mix it with one part vermiculite." I pointed to the bag. "And two parts finely ground peat moss." I nodded at another bag and lifted the can twice, one, two.

"If you need more, just make sure you use the same ratio. Then start adding water – a little at a time." And we were off.

"Cookie dough. Mix it to the consistency of cookie dough – smooth. No chocolate chips, no raisins."

This part usually brought out the inner child in the participants or maybe just the childishness. A misdirected

170

spray of the hose knocked off one of the men's caps. He gasped; the rest giggled. A lot of vigorous mixing and flicking of tufa chunks – into laps, across faces – ensued. The resulting "dough" of all that concentrated fun ranged from aged cheddar to cake batter.

"Now, you need a good three inches on the bottom, then start building up your sides. Two inches is best. You can put a can in the middle, help hold it in place." I started scooping my batch into a Tupperware cake-taker, working it, layering it with my hands.

The woman with the dog box looked at me and wrinkled her nose. Sliding a tablespoon of mud onto her trowel, she patted it with her fingers as if it were a stray threatening to do his business any minute. I reached over, dug in and dumped a hefty load into her box.

"You can use the back of your trowel instead of your hand, if you like," I said.

Except for the buzzing of carpenter bees, attempting to attack the rafters, and the slap of hands against wet mud and an exasperated sigh, quiet descended. We spent the best part of an hour, stirring, molding, pushing the mixture into the molds.

"Mine keeps sagging to the bottom. Maybe I'll just make a stump," said one woman as she plunged her fist into the mixture like punching down rising dough.

His shoulders slumped, Husband One looked over at Husband Two whose walls were at least five inches thick to his meager two or three. The wife of husband two peered inside his tufa tube. "You can plant one bean." She patted him on the back, leaving a cement handprint.

"Well, it might have something to do with cake batter versus cookie dough," commented another participant in her Elton John glasses and purple overalls hiked up over hefty knees.

By the time this class ended, sedition had turned into camaraderie. Good-natured heckling, a little backslapping, a shower of backhanded compliments followed us out of the barn and into a day of watery sunlight and champagne breezes.

As the two gentlemen heaved and loaded the dog box – heavier than ever with its load of hyper cement – into the back of her SUV, the owner, still perfectly coiffed, khakis and shirt pristine, thanked them with a grin. "I think I made a plant platter."

Harvey's Just Desserts

We've always preferred day-old chicks from a hatchery rather than our local feed store, where the choices were limited to great layers and excellent layers. Along with the bog standard, bred for laying chickens, hatcheries also deal in the quirky, the esoteric – Araucanas with their feathered mutton-chops and predilection for laying blue eggs; Polish top-knots with their Phyllis Diller hairdos and "Help! The sky is falling!" attitudes; CooCoo Marans stylishly feathered in storm cloud black overlaid with subtle brown markings; the French Dominique, Domineckers, as my grandmother called them.

And we always ordered sexed females. Wreaking havoc among the hens, roosters are notorious Lotharios, sly and brutal, serving no useful purpose in an egg-only enterprise like ours. Oh, but they can be handsome devils, like the one who sneaked past the hatchery inspector and ended up masquerading as just another girl chick among a carton of such chicks delivered to our local post office and brought home by a couple of unsuspecting hen keepers.

As an adolescent, Harvey – named for a family member who also strutted his stuff as if he was twice his size and good-looking to boot – plagued the hens with his constant juvenile attempts at a little amorous wooing. Proving more an aggravation than a suitor, the hens ignored him. But in time, he grew into the fine figure of a rooster he always knew he could be. Black and silver feathers glinting anthracite and diamonds in the sun, comb glowing cranberry red, this splendid example of a Wyandotte rooster walked among his hens like a sultan. Day by day, the wanton attacks upon his harem grew more and more bloody, the hens' backs looking like they'd escaped the plucking process in the nick of time. But a busy summer befriends a recalcitrant rooster and his bedeviling continued unchecked – for a time.

With more drop-ins than usual, teatime had been hectic. I needed more blueberries and more cheese, and at the moment, I was the most expendable. I headed across the garden toward the house and our back-up refrigerator. Another few minutes and the attack would have gone unnoted, unlamented. A hawk, spying the hole in the chicken netting – said hole having slipped its way down the fix-it list since last winter's heavy snows – flipped in mid-air and dove. His aim was perfect, the kill instant. But the hawk had given no thought to his escape route and now flapped against the netting, poor Harvey hanging from his talons. John, forced to do one of the few things he hates about life in the country, dispatched the hawk. Harvey lay bloodied and dead.

During the attack, the hens had cowered against the coop, trembling beneath the overhanging apple tree. I looked, counted. All there. They began to stir. Something was afoot.

174

They fluffed their feathers, began to mumble, milling around, reconnoitering. Suddenly, issuing a battle cry worthy of a general, they raced down the hill and flung themselves atop poor Harvey's carcass and set to, administering just desserts. Revenge was indeed a thing most sweet.

Josie the Great Protector

Even though we worked at shoring up the old hen house, nailing down a loose board, plugging up another raccoon-gnawed hole. Even though we buried the fence run a foot under ground and roofed the top with netting, fending off varmints proved a continual struggle.

Dawn still trapped between the mountains, I climbed Chicken Hill to collect the morning's eggs. Opening the door to the hen house, I looked in on a gaggle of still-roosting birds. I counted, as I did every morning. Eleven, twelve, thirteen. Wait a minute. I stepped closer, squinting, counted again. Twelve, thirteen. An absentee. Who? Phyllis, the flighty, dumb-as-a-stump, clueless Polish Top Knot. I called John. I took the hill behind the chicken house; John stepped over the electric fence onto the goat's hill. Walking all the way up to the spring, stumbling over old roots, plunging into gopher holes, I searched for that aggravating bird. Up at the spring, morning had fully blossomed, marred only by a missing chicken. I started back down, taking another track.

"Bobbie," John called, his voice pitched low, his tone calming. I hurried down the last twenty yards and over to the fence.

Josie had her particular lookout points and one was a rocky outcropping mid-way up the hill. That's where she lay, Phyllis limp in her mouth.

"Josie," I said, my heart sinking. She heard me, and when she did, she dropped that massive head and gently laid Phyllis on the rock at her feet. As soon as feathers touched granite, that harebrained chicken leaped up, ruffled her feathers, hopped off the rock and began pecking at dandelion fluff.

Josie considered all our farm critters her responsibility. She must have stood guard all night over that idiotic chicken.

Patron Saint of Babes and Blooms

And then there were the volunteers. Most didn't get beyond a phone call, "I'd love to work out in nature, with plants and all. Do you take interns? I'd work for just a place to lay my head under the stars and ambrosia to taste among the fairies." Or words to that effect. Volunteer number twelve, or so, showed up in work boots and a dress befitting Titania. I handed her a weeding trowel and fork and anchored her in a bed bristling in dandelions. But she kept wandering from her post, tripping over her velvet train every step or two, until she, eventually, wandered away.

Another, "Oh, how I would love to work here?" volunteer just looked at me when I passed her the mop and bucket. Left without a word.

And then there was Hannah. Hannah wanted to work for plants. Scaring the hell out of her patients at the women's clinic was her day job she said. "And I could use a little time around something not quite as brainless as some of the women I meet at the clinic." She gave a deep sigh and patted the fronds of a painted fern, so I figured she was talking about the plants.

A female Paul Bunyan, no task proved too arduous for her. If she said she'd be working four hours come Saturday, she toiled without a break until her allotted time had passed. When she finally raised her head - her smile reflecting great satisfaction - Hannah began her hunt. It might take until the afternoon mellowed into a farewell and doves cooed a goodnight from the rafters, but she'd come back to the shop, tired but serene, carrying a crate bouncing with plants.

Sometimes, I'd work alongside her, pulling weeds or deadheading or spreading a little compost. When we found our rhythm, the sun at our backs, waiting robins listening in, Hannah began to talk. More George Carlin than Robin Williams, she told her stories about the clinic, naming no names, with a deadpan delivery and an acerbic wit – laughing to keep from crying.

"Trolling in pairs, these girls. Had a couple in yesterday. Seventeen years old, one of them, and pregnant for the third time. Wearing short-shorts tight enough to require CPR. Baby-fat boobs in push-up bras. Big raccoon eyes swearing they didn't know how this happened, again." Looking where ridge top welcomed a low riding sun, Hannah sunk her trowel, then her hand, into the crumbling soil at her knees, let it sift through her fingers back to the earth, the giver of life.

"Then the one asked. No, she stood there in her trashy outfit, hot as a steaming compost heap, and demanded, 'I need more of them pills you gave me. Only, I want good ones that'll work this time.' " Hannah laughed. I laughed, the hawks crying overhead.

179

That day Hannah left with two, three-gallon old roses, fittingly called 'Vick's Caprice' and 'Cuisse de Nymphe.'

Sign Blind

Signs proliferated at The Herb of Grace as if it were a perpetual election season. The first, the "Private" sign, hung from our kitchen door when the shop still shared premises with our personal home, followed by the "Keep Out – Please" hanging about a foot from the floor. For good measure, I added a couple of private signs to the adjoining bedroom doors as well.

Someone would pry open a locked gate and up would go another sign. "Private" graced both the front and back doors to our home long after the shop moved to its own farmhouse. "Beware – Guard Dog" was nailed to the lower barn and kidding stalls after a couple, tugging at the barred door, managed a spectacular leap, Josie's teeth missing their haunches by inches. To our directional signs at the gate to the display gardens, we added "For The Herb of Grace Customers Only," after we watched a steady stream of tourists spill from their cars and buses, only to meander or hustle, according to their itineraries, into the gardens, then pile back into their various means of transport without a nod or glance at the shop, several clutching suspiciously sprouting plastic bags. We added, "All others $2.00 entrance fee. Refundable with Purchase." Nothing changed except for more heads ducked a little quicker, a little lower, as they passed the path to the shop on the way to their cars.

Kim swore "finger blight," as the British refer to it, increased when we posted the entrance fee.

I wished for a "Brazen Hussy" sign to hang around the neck of a clog-footed, denim-draped dowager carrying a glove full of stripped rose canes in her purpose-prepared baggies, pausing to snap seed heads off a rare *Agapanthus* at the shop steps. As she rolled from the parking lot, I saw brake lights brighten, car door open, gloved hand reach out, and as a last farewell, pull a strand of 'Glacier' ivy off the bank.

For privacy, we placed a wall of ridged tin vertical panels to separate the shop kitchen from the sales area. Access to the Verandah from the kitchen was guarded by imposing double cafe doors nine-feet-high. On hot days the cook set the top half ajar a few inches for ventilation. Closed doors and signs deterred only a few from poking their heads in and asking for another pot of tea. God bless them. Most just felt at home. And I felt glad, blessed even, that they chose to spend their day at The Herb of Grace, but I did wonder if "home" included a sink full of nasty dishes.

The sign maker and I stopped just short of hugging each other's necks when we met. I knew his kids' birthdays, their soccer teams. He recognized my voice and greeted my calls with, "Hi Ya, what'll it be today."

I told him, "I need a sign, no make it three. The usual white background, purple letters. 'No Dogs Allowed.' Wait, better make it four."

Ask any nurseryman or gardener or festival vendor what their number one pet peeve is and the majority will tell you, "Dogs. No, their owners." Dogs are fine – at home, or paws shackled together to avoid the hiked leg yellowing of a prized peony or *Hydrangea* or rose.

Most plant people are also animal people – dog lovers, cat and chicken lovers. But we know the destruction that even one small puppy can wreak with a well-aimed stream before strutting off to new adventures. I ended up with five "No Dogs Allowed" signs. John nailed one at the gate to the hoop houses, one at the nursery entrance to the gardens, another at the spring house entrance, one at the parking lot, one at the stone steps from the road, and the final one at the entrance to the shop gardens. They worked. Somewhat.

When we pointed at the signs while explaining, yet again, our no dog policy, most people understood and were gracious. One such couple ordered two French Teas and gave us an autographed Rosemary Verey gardening book. They commiserated over our dilemma and later shared an endearing memory. Upon their return home to Indiana, they sent us a thank you card. Inside were two photographs, one of Kim hoisting a pot of tea, the other of Duffy, our Golden Retriever, tongue lolling to the side, paws crossed, just hanging out at the foot of a white and purple sign – "No Dogs Allowed."

Invasion of the Chicken Snatcher

Six a.m. is early on an October morning. I rolled out of bed and punched the alarm. Shuffling into the kitchen, I felt for the percolator cord and plugged it in. Still muddled in sleep, I leaned over the counter and inhaled that first scent of comfort tucked in with the caffeine kick. I opened the refrigerator and removed two pounds of butter and laid them out on my eight-foot table rescued from some "downstairs" scullery. Reaching for the old white truck stop mug swinging from its hook, I poured my first cup, listening to the sputtered protest from the coffee pot.

I opened the kitchen window. Morning washed through with a Pinot Grigio chill, and the eastern sky blushed the colors of mangoes and peaches. Rustling through the leaves of the cherry tree, a Cardinal greeted the day's beginning. From the coop up the hill, I could hear the hens murmuring from their perch. The first of my family, waking up. Beneath the table, Duffy twitched and sighed, chasing rabbits in his dreams. I sat down at the table, took a sip of my coffee and eased into the day. This hour, my gift.

On goat hill, Josie barked. The chickens' murmur had turned into a decided grumble and in the next moment to a screaming hissy fit. I raced out of the kitchen and up the hill, stubbing my toe and falling headlong over the wheelbarrow I'd parked there the night before. With a decided hitch, I scrambled toward the now apocalyptic cackle emanating from the old hen house. Scrabbling for the latch, missing, trying again, I fought the door open and shined my flashlight toward the perches. Squinting into the beam with its tick-sized eyes, an opossum squatted one rung below my most histrionic Dominique, swooning with the vapors. At my "Hey!" the puffed- up rodent dropped from the perch and plodded away, disappearing into the cornered gloom of our ancient coop.

It could have played a chicken house in a Snuffy Smith comic strip, the one he always stole the chickens from, all weathered lumber, crumbling tarpaper still clinging to bits and pieces of it. A lot of people would have bulldozed the house, but it was there and had been for upwards of a hundred years. Longevity, it should count for something. How many eggs had been laid in the tilting nest boxes? How many chicken feet had scratched its powdered dirt floor? Besides, money was tight and time more so. We stapled poultry wire over the gaps between the boards to keep out the varmints and clear plastic come winter when good ventilation turned into frostbitten wattles and combs. And I told myself it had character. And 'Paul's Himalayan Musk' now climbed over the chicken run on its way to further clothe the coop in its fairy pink blossoms.

I flicked the flashlight toward the corner – no opossum – then checked our latest patch job. Still holding. Over the space of a few weeks, we'd bandaged a hole in the door, a crack in the siding, another crack in the siding, a hole in the overhead fencing and a hole in the outside fencing as first one varmint and then another lay in wait, planning its next maneuver. This latest slow-witted rodent followed on the heels of a wrestling match I'd broken up the week before between a black snake and the eggs destined for a spinach quiche.

Fully awake now, blood pumping, I headed back to the house.

I'd sautéed the red onion and added the spinach and was in the middle of whisking four eggs when the sound, finally, penetrated my brain. Again, blood-curdling clucks from up the hill. I took off at a dead run, side-stepping the wheelbarrow and yanked open the door. Inside, the beady-eyed opossum nodded up at me. Beside him lay our old girl. Over her six long years, she'd provided us with countless eggs and bushels of manure. She'd been born with a twisted beak and been bullied by the other chicks because of it. But it never slowed her down when it came to her Layena pellets. An inspiration for making the best of what you're given, she had held a special place in our hearts.

Somewhere in the recesses of its prehistoric brain, the murderer realized his predicament and scattered in a slow motion shuffle. By now, the sun peeking over the ridge provided enough light to watch him squeeze his football-shaped body between the outside wall of the coop and the backs of the nesting boxes.

Loading the rifle, I headed back up to the chickens, stepping around the wheelbarrow. Inside, I shooed the chickens into their run and locked them outside. I could hear the black-hearted scoundrel scratching between the walls, trying to further hide his evil heart.

In a fury, I fired the first few shots into where I thought he cowered. Then, I kept on firing because I realized I might just maim the poor little critter, and he might take a long time to die and I, alone, be guilty of his prolonged, agonizing death. So I kept going until I ran out of bullets.

John told me that evening, as he was prying off the outside boards of the coop to get to my kill, that a Marlin held 18 shots. I doubt the opossum suffered.

Behind the Blue Door

What about that door we found in the barn, the one we moved from one side to the other and back again? It stood there leaning between the 8-N and a hayfork, forgotten, while the goats had kids in the stalls below, while a hundred roses were potted off the back of our workhorse truck on the adjacent drive. Our second hypertufa class mixed peat and perlite in the foreground while it waited in the shadow, in the background.

Concentrating on the day-to-day, I passed it a hundred times without ever seeing it. Until one February morning when the weather hinted at May, I started working on a planting bed on the bank above the steps from the spring house to the garden path. Or what I saw in my mind as a path, but at the moment consisted of a wide expanse of grass, idle in its unremarkable approach to the gardens.

The breeze felt good, full of green smells and spring, as I shoveled compost, spreading it over bare earth. But I couldn't settle. The grass patch and its mob of dandelions grew uglier and more useless with every spade of soil I turned. It grew there as appealing as a spur-riddled sand patch or an asphalt parking lot wrapping a Wal-Mart? Driving by, customers would be anticipating a "buy one get one free" sale; a "one size fits all" bargain. Why work so hard on a garden, flowing with 'Pink Chintz' thyme, for it to end its journey at a weed-filled ditch bank?

I stood up, pondered. Stepped down onto the grass, walked a few paces, and stuck the spade into the sod equal distance from bank to road. Stepped back, squinted. Amazing. The upright spade changed the look, even the feel of the space, a vertical breaking a horizontal plane. But since the loss of my spade might prove a hindrance to the digging above, I set out to the barn to see what I could find.

I walked by the door several times, looking first at a coil of copper pipe, then a stack of culled, but bargain priced 4x4's, a couple of tobacco baskets, a bucket. I kicked at a pile of burlap bags. When the dust cleared and I could open my eyes, I stood looking at the door, solid yellow pine, five-paneled, tall and straight.

Snagging the post-hole diggers, I struck out across the growing area between two hoop houses, across the bridge, through the garden of Japanese maples and broke into a trot through the blueberry bushes to the waiting spade and the ugly grass.

Holes dug, 4x4 posts planted, shoulders aching, I wheeled the door over on my two-wheel barrow. Propping it up against one of the posts, I could sense the elements aligning. It would be beautiful. And it was. Painted blue, it hung, solitary, between its two gothic finialed posts, inviting all who came to enter to the gardens and the mysteries beyond. Planting the thyme on the bank would wait for another.

The Future Lies in the Past

Melancholy November. We had gloried in October's cerulean skies, adorned with its migratory flights. Seduced by the internal fires of autumn leaves, we thought maybe, this time, the light might last. But coquettish April's older sister, October, mysterious and more beautiful in her maturity, deserted us to a world bereft of luminous color.

Half-emptied nursery benches, seeming to lean into the courtyard wall for a little warmth, held a mongrel gathering of plants, looking despondent at not finding a home in someone's garden. Among them, a Portland Damask, 'Rose de Rescht', still holding to its cinnamon rimed leaves, scattered below its last heliotrope-tinted petals, looked especially forlorn. Earlier, it had been dumped out of its pot and then dumped back in by a woman who never had any intention of heeding the sign - "All plants 50% off. Fall the Best Time to Plant!"

She now sat on the Verandah awaiting her tea and scones, regaling her companions with the advice gleaned from some publication or another that it was perfectly okay to pop a plant out of its container and check its roots, make sure a garden center wasn't trying to "pull one over on you." Potting soil now peppered the gravel underneath my treasured rose, grown from a small cutting taken on a day of fine mountain mists. I breathed in, exhaled, and gave the devil her due. Exposed by the middle-aged vandal, the rose's congested roots needed a new home one size larger.

Outside hoop house one, nine 'Rose de Rescht' huddled, uncomfortable in their bulging 3-gallon pots. For four years since their beginnings as slivers off the old branch, they had grown and for three of those bloomed. Their tags, although faded, announced in bold type to anyone who would bend to read, "Blossoms of a hundred petals the color of young strawberries. Blooming throughout the whole of summer and into fall. Fragrance ambrosial." But lacking a glitzy marketing champion and bearing a name tricky to pronounce, they failed to attract more than a passing glance, quickly passed over for a media celebrity – 'Gertrude Jekyll', 'New Dawn', 'Lavender Lassie'.

For their faithful beauty, the Roses of Rasht, coastal city of the Caspian Sea, deserved a new home, a permanent home, a garden home in which to spread their long-suffering roots into rich composted loam. And I knew the place – a gentle slope that tilted toward the east and the rising sun, a lone blue spruce for a companion. I looked from the spruce back to the deep emerald leaves of the roses, and the beautiful composition of my imagination began to arrange itself.

Once in the ground, the roses would settle down, spreading new roots into the soil and blooming come May. What an impact nine would make tumbling down the hill, the bluesSpruce watching in wonder.

The vision perfect, the execution of my eloquent design, however, needed a team of stevedores, but at the time, there was only me. For five long weeks, between putting plants to bed for the winter, watering, ordering, calculating, I cut, shoveled, and carted grass off my little hillside. Then I dug the twice-as-wide holes, stirred in buckets of compost and smatterings of gypsum with the excavated clay. Placed one rose, then another. Ran down the slope, looked at the positioning. Ran back up, moved the first one over a fraction, and repeated said procedure nine times. Edited. Fine-tuned.

As December lumbered into January, Ruby came by and helped me spread mulch. In March, the *Muscari* and daffodils I planted between and around each 'Rose de Rescht' bloomed. In a few years, they'd naturalize the whole area. As the last of the 'Thalia' daffodils faded and drooped, the roses' emerald leaf nodes began to open, unfurl, glistening in the strengthening sunlight. Buds formed, swelled.

Nature orchestrated that first year's performance as an etude of three or four blooms, then a crescendo mounted as bud after bud burst to display the ripe, deeply rose, old damask blooms of 'Rose de Rescht'. Wading through the fragrance, first one customer, then a dozen clamored, "I want one."

It's not that I didn't know better. It's just that, once relegated to a back burner project, it remained there. And no one could have imagined that the garden of misbegotten roses would look like the first day in paradise. So the cuttings I scrambled to stick that evening in May would not be ready and flowering until next year.

Close to noon on the opening day of the Herb Festival, with the food booth piping out smells of cilantro, chili peppers, pita bread, bean sprouts, and tofu, I decided to play truant, go for a five-minute walk-about. These events had taught me the quick scan method for time conservation, and I was already three steps past the booth of our neighbor from up on Bluff Mountain before plant lust stopped me mid-stride. Long, slender, topped by a drop of thistle-purple bloom, she swayed above the crowd. A waft of taco-laden air thinned the pack, and I was left standing across the table from a weary looking Cheryl.

"What is this?" I ran my fingers up the stem, cradled the flower head between them.

"Well, it's a *Verbena*." She ripped a page from her receipt book and wrote out the name, *Verbena bonariensis*. "I brought a few to see if I could sell them."

I admit, close up in a 4-inch pot, they looked pitiful – lanky, roots humping to the surface, like a dwarf bald cypress minus the grace. Yep, convincing a customer to buy a starter pot of that mouthful might be a hard sale.

Like so many of the nurserymen we've met over the years, Ted and Cheryl were enthusiastic, slightly wacky in that way of all our Creek-dwellers and generous with their experience. When I bought a couple of the *Verbena*, Cheryl leaned over

194

in a conspiracy of neighbors and whispered, "Take some cuttings. The things root like a pig in truffles. Easy."

Divisions and cuttings from those two pots yielded a flat of *Verbena bonariensis* offspring in just a few weeks. By fall, a dozen flats in their stringy anonymity sat on the benches looking like something I needed to apologize for. The extras we planted in the garden didn't look much better, like skinny, oily ground elder. Untangling the bench dwellers from their sisters, setting them upright, again, onto their little plastic bottoms, turned into an hourly chore. Taking it personally, Ruby said, "Don't let anybody out the door without one."

For a while, we included a free Verbena with every purchase, until we noticed a customer slipping it into a tray of *Geranium* 'Lawrence Flatman' on her way to the parking lot.

Winter threatened, bullying its way with gale-force winds and pot splitting cold. Still in their black plastic containers, the remaining *V. bonariensis* died an ugly death to be resurrected as compost. In the garden, we slashed it to the ground, turned our backs and walked away.

March dawned and all hands – me and one commandeered daughter – geared up with rakes, spades, hoes, gloves, jackets, and to-go cups full of coffee. Ruby trucked wheelbarrow loads of gorgeous, newly-dumped, mulch downhill to the gardens.

Come spring and sprouting time, telling the difference between a prized perennial and a despised weed is neither art nor science, but a combination of both, honed by the familiarity born of a love for the ground you garden upon. A freshet of green, shimmering over bare earth, alerted me to the renewal of purple bellflowers. Looking around, I saw castor beans popping from their seeds to the soil's surface wearing an eye full of dirt and poppies spreading rumpled, silvery skirts.

Zoning into my springtime Zen state, I grubbed and dug and discarded. Noticing a splay of roseate leaves, I hoisted my spade to plunge it deep beneath an anticipated taproot – dratted dandelion. Seconds before annihilation, I halted. Hugged between its leaves, a crinkle of emerald foliage glistened. Sliding in my old hand trowel, I rocked it back and forth, loosening the root millimeter by millimeter. The dandelion pulled free. Tossing it into a bucket, I leaned over, nose inches from the ground - the *Verbena*.

As it grew, it plumped up, looking less like its former anorexic self – became a nice, utilitarian green presence. By mid-June, that green presence had turned into a windswept wave of amethyst, a purple haze swaying to a Joplin boogie, a mist of violet gems shimmering amidst the roses.

Since, it has been forever with me, prized filler in my gardens. A reseeder, it never seems to sprout where it will be unwelcome. And for those who can see beyond its awkward youth, it rewards the discerning. As customers strolled through the gardens during a rose-spiked May and June, a blue *Hydrangea* summer, a smoke-tinted autumn, *V. bonariensis* bloomed with abandon; I sold every one of those gangly ugly ducklings.

A Romantic and a Pragmatist Walked into a Garden

The couple arrived late summer, during that perfect year. Kneeling in the middle of the upper pathway, twins in their youth, they held hands – melting caramel blending with dusted cream. As I hurried past them on my way to the potting shed and the golden cluster of blooming, one-gallon 'Perle d'Or's' outside its door, I blinked a smile, gave a cursory nod. On my way back to the shop, wiping the rims of rose pots with the hem of my third garden apron of the day, muttering, "Hold on, hold on," I dodged the couple's backsides, scattering gravel, rushing on.

Two steps shy of the blue door, I heard her call, "Hi..." I turned. "Look!"

A few years back, on another day of making do with what we had, I'd levered a fat slab of granite from the rock pile above the chicken coop onto Kim's old Colorado toboggan and drug it down to the garden, the rock sometimes taking the lead. When we – the stone and me – slid to a stop side by side, I used a crowbar to heave it off the skid and onto the ground, and left it where it lay, and planted a garden of thymes around it.

I loved that rock. Like a wise old friend, it embodied presence and character, always there when I needed it – to contemplate a melancholy day, to rest when weary from too many dug holes, too many "Please and Thank Yous." And then I'd taken it for granted, in all my rushing, my busy-ness.

Now these two young people, interrupting my determined race with a look of amazement lighting their eyes, brought me back to my old comrade. Upon its back, in a depression like a water meadow in a far-off Lilliputian shire, a gathering of sun-splashed butterflies, the color of lemons, sipped nectar from the morning's dew. They stood then, two beautiful children with the sun on their faces and each other in their eyes.

"It's magical," she said.

"It's special," he said. "We're getting married today. At the Chapel. In Trust."

"May I pick my bouquet from your garden?" A breeze stirred her chestnut curls. Her eyes glistened.

What could I say?

Over at the shop a customer, impatient for her roses, dropped me back into my day. I grabbed the pots, glancing back once to the congregation of fluttering sunlight praying hallelujahs atop its ancient altar, and hustled away.

The betrothed dreamed their way through the garden until the seating of our last afternoon tea. As they approached the Verandah, I called out, asked if they had time for tea on the house before their ceremony.

"We do. And maybe a bite to eat?"

It was then I noticed the bouquet, held fast in their coupled hands. They must have stripped the 'Dark Lady' rose of all her voluptuous crimson buds, laid waste to a row of 'Provence' lavender, mutilated a pocket of wallflowers. A sprig of thyme, a wand of rosemary, seemed stingy, sprouting from such opulence.

A plate of scones, a round of Gouda, a baguette of bread disappeared, along with a pot of tea. The clock ticked past closing time, descended another twenty minutes when the bride-to-be held the bouquet to her nose, smiled, and asked, "Do I owe you anything for my flowers?"

After only a moment of calculation, I answered, "Yes," then quoted a price barely sufficient to cover the cost of a single pot of tea. After all, but for them, I would have missed the butterflies. But the pragmatist thought of the payroll still to make, and our late supper left-overs eaten to the last crumb.

A Gardener's Journey

A nother May, another Herb Fair, brought new faces.
"I'm celebrating."

Blonde hair radiating around her face like those old Bible
pictures of Saints, she stood there in her goldenrod-colored
shirt flecked with bits of mulch and macerating leaves.
Effervescent as a bottle of Fresca, she told her story in an
impassioned allegro. Thirty years of marriage – dead and
mourned and finally buried. And what to do with all that cried-
over compost? Plant a garden, an herb garden, of course.
"Where do I start?"

I asked her how big an area she wanted to cultivate. She
grinned. "The world, but I'll settle for the 200-square feet
outside my kitchen door. Right where his grill used to stand in
his precious lawn."

Her cargo shorts, streaked a crusty soil brown, lent visuals
to her claim that she'd already ripped out the grass and
"double-dug it with compost and gypsum, like I read about."

She made three trips to her car, mostly lavenders and
rosemary, some thyme, sage, cilantro. She also bought a bar of
linden soap and a fig bath oil for late at night, taken with a

glass of chardonnay. She left me with her address and phone number and the picture of her patting the heads of her lavender like they were puppies and stroking the rosemary like it had kitten ears.

I saw her again, later, on an early summer's day at The Herb of Grace. She spent the morning following, first Ruby, and then me around the garden, asking us to identify this tree – *Stewartia* – that flower – *Angelica gigas*. An antique tea rose, 'Sombreuil' and a *R. gallica*, 'Tuscany Superb', traveled back over the mountain with her to reign over her lavender hedge and encroach further into the lawn.

Every week that summer, she came for tea and spent the afternoon talking about gardening and, as often happens, moved on to discussions about life – the dreams of youth, the reality of life on the ground. How hard it could be and how funny. And how happy she was alone in her garden. Over the months, she wove her way into the fabric of The Herb of Grace.

Offering to teach a pressed flower class, she blew in on the day ahead of a thunderstorm with pressed pansies pasted to her blouse and dried heads of *Hydrangeas* pinned to her sandals. Tripping onto the Verandah, she dislodged her left *Hydrangea* head and managed to kick it between two balusters, scoring a hole in one and cackles from the half dozen participants sitting around the table. As she introduced herself, "I'm Merry!" the *Violas* began to disintegrate, dusting the floor with a potpourri of purple flakes, lightly scented. I'm not sure anyone learned to preserve the garden's beauty that day, but the teacher became a favorite.

The days of spring and summer disappeared in minutes, mystical and sublime, writing out their own sacred Book of Hours. And then one turning and then another and another until winter whispered, "I'm coming."

On a November Monday, late in the day, John and I and Kim – stopping by after a busy day writing copy for her artists – sat down to a supper of vegetable stew and hot from the oven flatbread. As he reached for the ladle and a second helping, John said, "Look!"

There she was, Merry, kneeling in a bed of *Amsonia* and 'Sweet Juliet' roses. Struggling to her feet, she dropped a fist full of ground elder into a purloined bucket, moved to a swarm of *Alchemilla mollis*, Lady's Mantle in waiting, and knelt once more. We watched from the window, the three of us, standing, looking out, like voyeurs, zookeepers held hostage by a weeding hominid, female variety. Feeling conspicuous, backlit by the kitchen light, we ducked. Sitting back down to a stew grown cold, we left her to it – bowed head, hands bleeding sap the color of leaf and stem, holding a rose the color of autumn, faithful 'Penelope.'

Merry left in a dark so profound she might have been a wraith, moving through the garden to her car. I never saw her again, and to my shame, I didn't notice, not for a long time. Not until a newsletter returned, stamped No forwarding address.

In the Nursery

Pride Cometh Before a Fall

Every opening, every spring brought a scramble for help. A few of the help became valued employees. A handful became family. There were gems and a few hockey pucks. What with the new shop and all that entailed, we needed gems.

She flopped down at a table and motioned her friend to sit. It was my day to be "pie lady," * and I was taking server duties. I smiled and lifted the teapot.

"Tea? On the house." I said.

"No. I'm here for a job." She planted her boots, rested her fists on her cargo-panted knees, and leaned in as if waiting for the bell to signal round two.

Over at the potting shed, Carl Junior lugged 70-pound bark bags from the barn to the shed, dumping them into the mixing table, counting his hourly wage in minute increments on the way to just enough for his senior prom. Abby, aka Moonbeam, my rehire from the last two springs, funneled soil into quart pots, bumping up rosemary liners. She'd been at it for at least an hour and was due to wander off any minute.

Ruby had her hands full, both in the figurative and literal sense, spreading mulch. Kim multi-tasked – at the counter alternating between helping customers, writing a press release, and brewing tea. In there somewhere, she tweaked a brochure for one of her clients. Yes, I could use a few more ready hands and strong backs.

"I need help in the nursery houses, basically watering, weeding. Maybe eight till two. I can pay fifty cents over minimum wage to start."

She snorted, "I don't think so," made to rise from the table, huffed, and sat back down. "I made twice that at Ricola."

Didn't they make cough drops? In the Alps?

"Sorry. That's what I pay. Maybe a bit more for someone with experience."

"I was in charge of sages." Spittle flecked the old damask tablecloth. Her nostrils flared. Spiked hair aggressed.

Never a wise idea to hire someone you'd really rather throttle. So what did I do?

"One week. At a dollar over minimum. Trial only. Then, we'll see." I said.

I watched her stroll away. Outmaneuvered. I, Huckleberry Finn, paintbrush in hand, a mile of metaphorical fence at my back, watched her stroll away. An old country saying passed through my mind, the one about blood from a turnip, which was about where I'd have to look to come up with that extra dollar.

Day one. She arrived late. At a pace to rival a winter sun, she slogged through the garden, across the bridge, past the stock beds, and met me at the door of the poly tunnel where our newly-potted babies get coddled while their tender roots stretch and grow to adolescence.

"Do you have any idea how long it takes to get way out here?" She was dressed for combat, almost – fatigues, flight jacket, cap, and Birkenstocks.

"You'll have to move your car." I pointed to the cars parked next to the barn then toward hers. "The parking lot is for customers. Different shoes?"

For three hours, she straddled a bucket of diluted bleach water and washed pots. She stretched a forty-five-minute lunch break to an hour and a half, then straddled the same bucket for another three hours. After she drove away fifteen minutes early, I walked over to her workstation. Two-quart pots still bobbed in the swill left from her day of washing up.

Day two. Arrived less late. Taking her to the hoop house, home to flats of culinary herb seedlings, I demonstrated the basics of good watering, holding the nozzle below the leaves at the base of the plant and keeping the flow low as appropriate for these toddlers.

"Try to keep the leaves dry and water each one until the water comes out of the holes at the bottom. Watering is the most important job in a nursery and the hardest one to do right," I said.

"I know how to water a plant." Each word, heavy with disapproval, dropped into her deep well of umbrage.

Down an employee, Carl Junior sleeping in, the morning passed in a series of sprints between the shop and the Verandah, the plant tables and the growing beds. Before our lunch reservations started to arrive, I jogged across to the tunnels to check on the new hire. I stepped into the hoop house. Flat after flat of little heads drooped, their baby feet parching in pots of peat dust. A shower of tepid water sprayed me in the face. The fount of experience, waving the wand in an arc high above the tables as if directing a silent symphony, stood transfixed, eyes closed.

Courting lawsuit and injury, I grabbed her six-inch bicep and marched her over to her Datsun.

Cramming twenties, a large portion of the day's receipts, into her hand, I said, "Trial's over."

We saw her again. A few weeks later, on an afternoon washed new by a shower of rain, her Datsun, power steering screeching, pulled into the parking lot. She climbed out. Flattened by the rain, her hair hung in little ducktails around her face. She'd rolled up the legs of her cargo pants and shed the flight jacket. Her t-shirt yodeled "Ricola!"

Walking to the small, gated enclosure marking the entrance to the gardens, she slumped onto the massive boulder outside the springhouse door, oblivious to the small pool of rain held like an offering in the carved surface of the stone. Jewel-blue *Corydalis* puddled between the rocks. Japanese painted fern brushed the walkway. Sunlight glistened on every green thing. She dropped her head into her hands and did not leave until the sun slid behind Craig's mountain.

* The Pie Lady is a character in an engrossing Dean Koontz book, *From the Corner of His Eye.*

Like so many of his books, this one left us feeling weirdly hopeful.

Troubled Wayfarer

Many intrepid souls found their way over the mountain to The Herb of Grace, the small nursery, shop, gardens and tearoom harbored in the middle of nowhere – some of them in want of a job. And since this horticultural enterprise owned me for an innumerable number of hours over a goodly number of years, I met each prospective employee with hopeful anticipation. A treasured few proved truly unforgettable.

He arrived, rattling into the driveway in his old Chevy stepside. Stepping out of the cab, he announced, "I'm Calvin, and I just love flowers and growing things. And I'm a hard worker." He slapped the pinned-up leg of his khakis with the flat of his hand. His prosthesis, so he said, rode around in the back of his truck. "It just gets in the way."

He'd survived Vietnam only to come home and lose his leg from the knee down in motorcycle "foolishness."

In a voice accented with pure Tarheel, he told me he was Melungeon, a race mixed and stirred from three continents and dumped onto the Piedmont of North Carolina. Though his face looked weathered by tribulations of one sort or another, his eyes gleamed the crystalline green of coral reef waters off the coast of Big Key, fathoms deep.

His first day at work, he drove up just as sunlight baptized the trees up on the hillside, carrying his own worn spade and pruners. "They fit me."

I took him to a part of the garden being overrun with romping *Campanula glomerata* 'Joan Elliot'. Badly in need of digging and potting on for resale, the little beauties would have to wait for another day. Calvin's assignment was their companions, a dozen roses in need of a pruning. I started to demonstrate the proper technique, but he was ahead of me. With the instinctive touch of a man of the soil, he reached for a cane and snipped it cleanly toward an outfacing bud. I left him to it.

The sound of his old truck echoing off the valley walls woke me earlier and earlier every morning, until I stepped outside one day, before dawn and – worse yet – before my first coffee, to plead, "Not before six!"

What breaks he took consisted of a swallow of sweet tea from a jug he kept under a nearby shade tree. For Calvin quitting time came only after the last of his babies were in the ground, tamped down and dosed with a good helping of manure tea. No dusk to dawn lights ever shone at The Herb of Grace, only stars. If they had, midnight may have found him still cussing the burdock for bullying his peonies. One of the best natural plantsmen I'd ever met, he seemed to sense – inhaling a flower's breath, listening to its rustling leaves, his fingers tasting the soil – the needs of his botanical kingdom.

A few weeks into his time with us, the morning blustering toward noon, I watched him weave his way across the bridge from the gardens and into the potting shed, his work bucket swinging from one arm.

Behind me, I heard Shirley, a volunteer working for plants, yell from the sale benches, and I turned to walk back to the shop along a path lined with a congregation of *Achillea.*

"How many hours worth?" She asked as I approached and frenzied negotiations ensued.

A half-hour later found me at the garden's blue door looking across to the nursery. Calvin, using the wheelbarrow as support, was hitching his way back to the thatch of 'Joan Elliots'. Inside the barrow potting soil cushioned a rack of 4-inch pots, a 3-gallon container for weeding, and his tea jug. Depositing his load beneath a dogwood, he turned his face to the sky. I could feel him smiling a garden away. Sitting in a river of crinkled green, fat buds near to bursting, he dug and potted and watered the *Campanulas*, stopping every now and then to tip the jug. Waiting long enough for me to get around to teasing out the bellflowers, he'd set about the job himself.

I awoke one morning at the tail end of September just as dawn was working its way along the valley floor and made my way out to the hoop houses – my first cup of coffee in hand. Here among the pots and the bags of soil and the herbs and the roses and the green and lovely things, I found the true jump-start to my day. I heard a rustling from the barn, the bats bedding down. With its triple grace note, a Cardinal greeted the day. Then the humming of bees and the shushing of bluebirds ushered in the solitude of early morning. I started the day's watering.

A car door slammed. I looked up to see Ruby, my good right arm, crawling from her Subaru. Untangling two 'Betty Cornings' in a row of *Clematis,* I looked up to see Calvin's truck pulling into the drive. I glanced at my watch. Late for him. He stepped out onto his one leg, steadying himself as usual, one hand on the doorjamb. This time he continued to sway, gave up and slid down onto the running board, his crutch clutched between his legs. Dropping the 'Betty's' onto the ground, I hurried over to see if I could help. I smelled him before I got there, the aroma of day-old whiskey seeping from his pores. You don't get that sour mash odor from the occasional bender. This was a long time in the making – crouching horrors at midnight, waking to swales of hell the morning after.

He worked in the shade that day, wearing sunglasses. His hands trembled as he pulled grass knotted between blades of blue flag iris. Sweating 100-proof Kentucky, he punished himself by weeding the gravel walkways. At noon, Ruby asked him if he wanted something to eat. He said he couldn't stomach it. On the hill, Josie, our Great Pyrenees, stood and stretched, preparing to gather her goats and herd them home for their evening feed. I found him behind the barn, forking compost.

"Calvin, it's after seven."

With a face all ashes and despair, he looked over at me. "I was late coming in."

There were still good days, lots of them, but the bad hounded him, piling one atop the other. It was a time of heartbreak for him and for me. Then one day he failed to come to work at all. A week passed with the gardens missing him, his pinks and his roses looking pinched and forlorn.

A gracious morning more than a week later, his wife climbed out of his old pick-up. Parked in its usual space at the barn, it looked at home, but somehow lonely. Julie, sweet-faced and mannered, like her mama taught her, tried to keep her voice from stumbling over the words.

"I come to pick up Calvin's check. He's not doing too good and we got him up at the VA. I don't know if he'll be back."

She drove off then back up the mountain, carrying his check and a little extra from the register. Pressed upon her in a life already burdened, one of his cosseted 'Joan Elliots' and a young 'Lavender Lassie', his favorite rose, rode along.

"Damned useless thing to do." I swiped my eyes and headed through the bellflower bed and home.

We Could All Use a Little Fairy Dust

We met Richey first. He pounded out leaves of bronze on a form carved from oak as hard as iron for our friends, the fountain builders. Later for the new shop, he scaled ladders to carry and nail into place sheets of drywall that weighed more than he did. And he promised us a window of glass, leaded in rainbow colors, to grace the gable – facing east to welcome the light.

While he had sojourned upon this earth long enough to leather and toughen, he had chosen for a wife a young thing, tinier even than him, delicate, fragile. Tinker Bell to his Gimlet.

She perched in the passenger seat of their old Datsun truck – stitched with wire weaving the rust together. Next to her sat a little girl, eyes luminous like a baby wren, strawberry ringlets clinging to her skull – mirroring her mother.

"This is my wife, Pearl. She's really good with flowers."

Pearl leaned forward, plucking a squirming toddler from her breast, his arms and legs thrashing, looking for all the world like Pinocchio coming to life.

"Hello." Her voice was a whisper, her smile dreamy. She wore floral overalls and a lace- edged t-shirt, her feet bare.

I sighed. Just what I needed, another aspiring earth mother sprinkled with a little fairy dust. The type seemed to proliferate in this neck of the woods, and I'd made their acquaintance more times than I wished. Sweet and harmless, a little too earnest in their ever-changing life roles, making them just about useless as employees. The child attached itself again and began feeding as if devouring its mother, reducing her to a sprite of bone and skin.

I kept my mouth shut and waved them away back down the road.

From the first, the neighborhood's friend in need, Millie, told us she'd pave the way for us. "Don't you worry. I'll be around in case you hit a snag, need some advice."

And she was, always.

That's how I ended up on one of my precious Mondays off, traveling down the highway toward Betsy's Gap, Millie riding shotgun.

Roy lived up on a hill with his wife in a new double-wide with central heat and air and a dishwasher, just off the highway a few miles up from the cafe. "But he grew up in his mama's house, just like she did. His great-granddaddy cut the chestnut and poplar from a stand up the ridge, planed it as smooth as a buckeye, built a house for his wife, no more'n a teenager, and their mess of kids."

No way he could sell it with that kind of history so he'd rented it to a couple of foreigners. "New York or California, someplace like that. Babes in the woods, anyway, renting a house with nothing but a kerosene heater in it."

Now he had all his mother's belongings to get rid of. "His mama has some old bowls. I know you like old bowls." So Millie said.

Sheltered within a locust grove, the house seemed to slumber, caught up in a tale by the Brothers Grimm, forgotten. The only sign of a human tale, the red curtain flapping through an open window.

Tin roof, single story painted a faded brown so ugly it must have been a store return, the house was a puzzle of add-ons, each bearing witness to a family line eroding along fault lines of poverty. I pulled the Subaru up to the back porch and cut the engine, looking out at the house. Waiting there, framed in a rectangle of listing posts and sagging rafters, stood the renters – Pearl with succubus and child – waving enigmatically, inviting us in.

They must have lived in shadow on the brightest days, sunlight unable to carve an entrance through the thorny hedge of locusts. And the cold, even in May, penetrated my bones, threatening chilblains. The infamous kerosene heater, a quarter the size of the room, blazed away, warming the air in its own six-foot circle. Stepping away from it to the table where Mama's bowls waited felt downright sacrificial. Stacked atop a red-checkered oilcloth that looked like it arrived in a shopping bag from F. W. Woolworth, circa 1950, stood a meager collection of chipped Pyrex bowls and one banded McCoy.

The McCoy traveled back up the mountain to the shop. So did Pearl.

Kim's Mazda pulled in as Ruby and Pearl started up the gravel walk, and she caught up with them at the steps to the Verandah, all three dragging.

For the first time since emptying the coffee pot and turning on the oven that morning, I sat down at a table only mildly derelict after the day's merrymaking, propping my feet on a neighboring chair. The real disaster hid behind closed doors, ripening in a stacked sink. My jaw ached from telling the story of The Herb of Grace for the hundredth time, the story of tea for the fiftieth, and the care of old roses for - I didn't remember. Overhead, a carnival of crows harassed a hawk across a sky milky in the dying light. I commiserated. And as much as I loved my shop, I envied Ruby and Pearl's dirty knees, their green and grimy hands. I envied Kim's day of composing, writing in a silent room. She called, "Hey, don't you ever work." I snarled and ducked back inside for the checkbook.

By the time I returned to the table, Kim had already retrieved the left-over teacakes and put the kettle on to boil. While I wrote checks, Kim poured tea - Orchid Oolong. Pearl sipped, "This is good." She could talk.

As I handed over her first payday, I asked, "Would you like to work in the shop for me sometimes. If you're serving, you get tips. And it's cleaner." I nodded at the soil and twigs she'd shed around her chair.

She did think about it for a minute, I'll give her that. When she answered, though, I realized there had never been a chance. "No. I mean, not really. I don't like being around people much. I prefer the plants."

Freshening her cup, I pushed a teacake her way.

"I love my job. I didn't know I would. Well, this is my first job really. I left with Richey the day I graduated from Caltech." As if amazed at the incongruity, the strangeness of it all, she laughed, shook her head, setting ebony curls bouncing. "A master's degree and this is my first ever paycheck."

An oddity all right, this place, this Creek, surreal even. A marine biologist pressing apples, a professor flipping pancakes, and a graduate of Caltech weeding tomatoes, passing teacakes as fireflies flickered around us.

It took weeks, the summer, to put flesh on the story of Pearl.

An only child of wealthy parents, Pearl, defiant for the first time in her life, absconded with a carpenter-artist-vagabond named Richey, fifteen years her senior. They crossed the country looking for a mystical little valley, a realm far removed from the one they left behind.

"It still doesn't seem real." She said one morning, turning to look at Kim, who was helping deadhead a 'Madame Alfred Carriere' rose. "I wonder sometimes if I'm lost in somebody else's life."

We heard the rest from Ruby, picked up at the mulch pile, in the vegetable garden spreading compost, weeding among the roses, this tale full of pathos. Pearl's babies had been sick a lot last winter with runny noses, coughs, fevers.

"Wind blows through that house as if the walls were spun from spider webs."

On the day of first frost, Ruby told me, "Pearl's really dreading the coming cold."

And later, while she and Ruby stacked pots of hellebores and Japanese painted ferns inside their winter home, Pearl told her that her mother had sent tickets and money "to come home to California. For me and the kids."

Love lost out to the bitter cold and the health of her babies.

Soon after, Richey began to wander, tetherless without his Pearl, to other places. During that winter of heavy snows and Arctic temperatures, the valley mourned the loss of four sweet souls. Under the locust trees, the little house stood empty, whistling its solitude through the cracks.

An Old Rose Primer

Old Roses. They grew the heart of this nursery. Years ago, when Kim was a toddler, I planted one, a Bourbon, 'Mrs. Paul', offspring of a very famous French lady, 'Mme. Isaac Pereire'. Mine, rooted from a cutting taken at an old cemetery outside of St. Augustine, Florida, bloomed her second year in early May. When the buds began to swell, Kim paid it a visit every morning and at the end of each day, tiny hands clenched tight, struggling against temptation. At last, a morning drenched in sunlight coaxed it into bloom. I witnessed the encounter as I stepped from the kitchen. Kim, standing enraptured, chin level with the first nodding bloom. "Mama, Mama it's ripe!"

A memory carved deep in this mother's soul – child and rose, both blushing the pink of a morning sky.

Years later, I read of the rose rustlers traveling the south, rescuing forgotten roses from roadsides, abandoned farmsteads and graveyards – sacred spaces. In Hope Cemetery near my mother's house in rural Florida, an old noisette kept rosy watch over a little girl, planted there by a mother haunted at having to leave her baby all alone. Homesteading on a ditch bank somewhere between Birmingham and Montgomery, another lost rose, signaled a passing car for a ride to a new home.

With the rose, the history is long, steeped in mystery and intrigue, its determination to survive legendary. Even in the midst of war, Josephine was allowed her roses, an explorer, his. And so it seems, even a farm wife — or a shopkeeper — can share a love of a 'Souvenir de la Malmaison' with an Empress or a 'Gold of Ophir' with a Fortune.

Through the years, camellias have seduced me, like Alice, with wonder. I've succumbed to the siren calls of lavender. But old roses? They speak to me of eternity.

Kindred Spirits in Unlikely Guises

It was brewing a hot one, as it can some days, even in the Appalachians. Feet sweating inside my clogs, I headed back to the shop after identifying yet another "little green plant with a little pink flower" on the far side of the garden. As I ducked between the spring and smoke houses, a brand new, metallic, midnight blue Lincoln pulled into the parking lot. The driver got out, straightening the crease in her chinos. Wearing one of those visors I always associate with golf, she turned and twirled her fingers in the air like the Queen summoning her three ladies-in-waiting. They scurried in behind her like chicks in the wake of mama hen as she sailed toward the Verandah.

"Oh boy," I muttered.

And then she turned around and shamed me. She had as many freckles as wrinkles and her grin exposed a gap between her front teeth — no well-heeled matron, this one. She held out her hand, one of our rose lists tucked in her shirt pocket.

"Hello. Oh, I am so glad to be here." Her accent was pure Tar Heel, generations long. "We're here to buy roses."

"Oh good," I said, and she handed me a postcard of a Judas tree, sunlight spraying through its branches. I turned it over. *Morning in Brookside Gardens.*

"It's lovely. Where is it, Brookside? I'm sorry, I don't think I've heard of it," I said.

"Not enough have, and we want to change that."

Shorter by inches, rake thin in emerald green linen, the next woman spoke. "We're part of a group working on bringing the gardens back to life, and we're starting with the rose garden." She gestured, and I noticed her swollen knuckles, chipped fingernails – whole, long days in the garden.

A third, with short gray hair brushing deep-set eyes, pointed at each of the others in turn. "Anne, Hetty, Nan" and then tapping her chest, "Ronnie."

"Are you Grace?"

It's a question I was asked at least once every day, so I just smiled and said, "Actually, I'm Bobbie, but I'll answer to Grace anytime."

The idea of restoring a lost gem, a private garden made public in the early half of the twentieth century, lit their faces, turning their enthusiasm into poetry. In spite of the problems facing so many botanical spaces – lack of revenue, lack of marketing, lack of knowledgeable help – they had formed a group of volunteers, close to fifty in number, who were working to acquire new stock, put out the word, and just plain pull weeds.

They'd picked us for their roses. Astonished and grateful, I told them, "I'm honored."

Morning melted into afternoon as we discussed the merits of the repeat-blooming bourbons versus the once-blooming *gallicas*, considered by many to be the finest of the old garden roses. We talked of fragrance – the Tea roses mythically scented by the Oolongs, the Darjeelings as they shared cargo holds on the clipper ships sailing from the Orient in the days of the British East India Company; the Sweet Briar, *Rosa eglanteria,* whose foliage smells of green apples in the sun; the damasks, cultivated in Persia, carrying in their petals the fragrance of, well, old rose.

Over cups of jasmine tea, I told them the story of 'Old Blush', the first remontant rose to sail from China to Europe in 1752, and on from there to the bay of Charleston. And found, again, centuries later in a graveyard in rural Alabama, its pale pink petals drifting among the stones and the memories.

Hetty noticed, first, the shadows growing over the floor, climbing the walls. "Good Lord, we've got to get home."

They left with fifteen 3-gallon roses, packed pot to top into the trunk of Anne's Lincoln, among them an 'Old Blush' and a sweet 'Eglantyne'.

A Rose by Any Other Name Would Heal Complete

Maneuvering around and up the pathway, I ducked my head, smile plastered in place, trying hard not to engage with any of the garden visitors milling about. Ashamed of myself, I sunk my head even lower, but I knew a quick "hello and welcome" could lead to thirty questions and half an hour; and I was on my way to the barn to see if I truly did have one more three-year-old Apothecary rose in the growing bed. With tempers rising, sarcasm turning toxic between two warring members of a visiting garden club, I needed the rose to restore peace. As I left the shop, the rest of the members had started picking sides, aligning allegiances.

No one to blame but myself, I'd instigated the rivalry, weaving the tale of the "Red Rose of Lancaster," the Apothecary rose, and the "White Rose of York."

"More than seven centuries have passed since the duke chose the red rose and the king the white."

From the winter of 1450, or thereabouts, to the spring of 1485, civil war – the War of the Roses – ebbed and flowed.

"Onto the battlefield at St. Albans, the duke's men rode in wearing the *Rosa Alba semi-plena* as their badge of allegiance. From across the valley, the forces of King Henry VI charged in, *Rosa gallica officinalis* pinned to their tunics."

Abetting the looming skirmish, the Rose of Lancaster perched on top of the stonewall outside the creamery, resplendent in her crimson-purple finery, her golden stamens sparkling in the sun and her powerfully evocative fragrance perfuming the air around us. Before the echo of my history tutorial faded, the woman named Lee-Ann laid her claim, "It's mine." And reached for it.

Next to her, Harriet grabbed, snarled, "I said it first." She said, squaring off for the next engagement on the horticultural battlefield of our own war of the roses.

Passing through the arbor intent on my reconnaissance in the rose fields, I spotted a woman alone on her knees in a mound of 'Bath's Pink' *Dianthus*, a rose blossom cupped between the palms of her hands. She looked up as I passed, and I smiled much like Nicholson's Joker as I increased my pace. An unnecessary maneuver; whoever she saw it wasn't me. Across the bridge, I slowed, grabbing a five-gallon pot from the stack leaning against the potting shed.

The digging took only minutes, the spade crumbling the rich dark earth as it sliced through, and I was soon retracing my steps back across the bridge, past the massive syrup kettle where we host our bonfires, up the stone steps to the gravel path. The almost identical (Please, God) Apothecary resting on my aproned hip like a toddler, my mind racing ahead to the confrontation, to the next sale, to tomorrow's task, I almost stumbled over her. Still on her knees, a praying Madonna, she stood as I started past.

"What's her name?" She nodded at the rose at her feet.

"His. He's 'Comte de Chambord'." And I looked at her, and for a fragment of time, I stopped my frantic flight. Lit by the sun streaming through the maple leaves fluttering at her back, she seemed, almost, to be shining between my world and another.

"And that one." This nod directed at the pot in my arms."The Apothecary rose," I said and she shifted, slightly, and the light moved with her. And I didn't talk, then, of wars, but of the rose's other stories, her other histories.

"It was planted in the gardens of the great monasteries, and the fragrance of its blossoms used to heal those troubled in mind and spirit."

"Ah." I watched her look around and steady her gaze upon the mountains. "I can feel it. Here in your garden. The healing. Peace. My first. Thank you." Then she looked at me, and I saw her eyes – blue windows of such sorrow.

"I drove from Atlanta this morning. Running away." Again, she smiled.

"I lost my daughter one year ago today. She'd been struggling, troubled for months, but the morning before her accident she called me. Told me how everything was better, how good she felt. Then she laughed, the little girl I'd so missed. Said she was coming to see me. She never made it home." All those questions with no answers.

228

I said, "I have a daughter and I can not imagine." I stretched out my hands, took hers and for long moments we held to each other around an Apothecary rose.

I wish I'd thought then to give it to her. The rose. But I didn't think. I didn't think until I set it on the ground between the two combatants. "Here it is. The Apothecary rose, ancient and healing."

"Is that the same as Lee Ann's? Exactly?"

Dear God, it would have been so much happier in Atlanta.

An Arbor is Born

On a passably pleasant day in February, John and I met at opposing corners of our first hoop house sited next to our original driveway. Armed with razor knives, we pierced the heavy mil plastic sheathing – rendered useless from too many seasons in the sun – and stripped it free of its galvanized skeleton. The piped ribs, silhouetted against the low winter sun, looked caught in some middle ground between past and future.

It had irritated me all last season, that 10 x 20 foot growing house. Feeder plants resided there, waiting their turn on the display benches outside the shop – *Campanulas, Monardas, Dianthus*, green things hungering for adoption. But their companions now lived beyond the gardens, across the bridge in new planting beds and bigger, more up-to-date hoop houses. And no one ever seemed to remember the pinched and prettied plants, waiting for their debut under their sweltering plastic roof – until they drooped. They needed to be where the workers, well, worked.

And the hoop house no longer looked sturdily utilitarian there in the middle of the gardens. It looked downright seedy, like ragweed among lilies.

John saw it first, the potential. "How about an arbor?"

A Giverny-like arbor for our customers to stroll through, shadow and light, paradise blooming overhead. I trotted across the bridge to rob the growing beds.

A happy, *Vitis vinifera purpurea* is a glorious thing. Deeply lobed leaves emerge green in spring with tints of cool burgundy. With the advent of summer, the color becomes more pronounced, saturating the leaves in a crimson glow. Autumn brings fruit. Infatuated, I saw only its beauty, dreamed of tasting its succulent harvest. Only later would it reveal its black-spotted heart (and leaves). I planted two, one on either side.

To twine and drape across both entrances, I chose a *Clematis viticella* 'Polish Spirit.' By the second year, it had grown into a tapestry of rich purple velvet and verdant green silk over the entrance to the pergola. Rambling 'Veilchenblau' roses and shell pink 'Hagley Hybrid' *Clematis* clambered over the sides and across the roof. In the fall, Kim deposited bulbs of *Muscari* 'Valerie Finnis' and *Narcissus* 'Thalia' into the black loam at the feet of the climbers.

When we began the removal of the black woven ground cover of the former hoop house turned pergola, I found tiny rosettes of foxglove, poppy plantlets, bellflower babies, growing along the frayed edges of the ground cloth. Down on my knees, I cut around them, pulled them free of their bondage. Then, I covered the nursery of exposed plants with floating row cover to protect them through the end of winter. Under cover, without interference by human-kind, the tiny plants spent the cold days and colder nights stretching their roots into an Eden all their own.

The season opened with the new arbor garden looking a little sparse, like scattered children on a playground, but our loyal customers encouraged us with a smile and a two thumbs up accolade. And during a spring of just enough rain and a summer of the perfect blend of sun and shadow, the garden flourished. Forgotten were the cold blasts of last winter, the dry days of fall. Instead, we danced in the moment of blessed growth.

A Floral Namesake

I recognized the signs – averted eyes, tentative smile – of a listener. I've worn them all my life, these marks of the socially challenged. I stepped nearer, trying not to spook her, and said, "Hello, and welcome." I offered her a cup of Black Currant tea.

Shy, like a skittish fawn, she backed away, whispered, "Oh, no. That's okay."

I left her then, to look around. Dragging the water hose, my extra limb, to a table of *Geum rivale*, I poked the nozzle under the leaves and turned the indicator to flood. A couple, dressed in the wide-legged shorts and collared shirts of vacationers, asked, "What are you doing?"

Squelching the obvious answer, I pulled out a tag, handed it to the man, "It's called the water avens. Likes moist soil." I plucked it out of his hand as he reached toward his pocket and stuck it back into the pot. Across the bobbing heads of a trio of English roses, 'Perdita', blooming their little apricot hearts out, my shy visitor was looking my way, grinning. Ducking her head, she lost herself in a row of 'Higan' cherries, the trees' rich, burnished, mahogany bark reflected in the glow of her face.

A customer poked her head out of the shop, "I'm ready." We had a good visit, Lisa and me, over her purchase of her usual Black Currant tea and her jar of lavender honey and her impulse buy of a bird bedecked tea towel. But plants called me back to the watering.

I startled her, the shy faun, as I rounded a display of ferns and mosses, gazing mesmerized at a fanfare of *Clematis.* With the tip of a finger, she brushed one fat, silky bud, set it to bouncing on its delicate green tether.

She bought something that first day. I don't remember what. A few days later, she returned.

"Hello, good to see you." Again, I offered tea. This time she reached for the cup, a smile teasing her eyes, and said, "Thank you."

She didn't stay long, a quick visit to the gardens and then back she came to the table of *Clematis.* Stroked, I swear, the same bud, fatter now, bulging at the seams showing a swell of blush pink undies.

Busy serving – a table of four French Teas, a three top Cream Tea – I looked up a couple of days later to see her arrive and walk directly to her post of the earlier visits among pots of *alpinas, tanguticus, viticellas, montanas,* and the gaudily glorious blooms of the large flowered hybrids. She touched her lips, placed her hand over her heart, then turned and fled back to her car.

Intrigued, I set a pot of Imperial Gunpowder in front of a young man in cargo shorts and a Mama Gaia t-shirt and walked down the steps to the display tables. I passed 'Nelly Moser', 'Betty Corning', and a riot of purple 'Polish Spirit' *Clematis* and approached the corner where sat her favored plant.

Then the aroma hit me, that rich combination of Madagascar vanilla spiked with a soupcon of clove. The swelling bud, with its siren song, had opened to the sugar-dusted blossom of *Clematis* 'Mayleen'.

I was snapping off the spent heads of 'Butterfly Blue', *Scabiosa columbaria*, keeping an ear out for yet another new hire and her constant queries of, "what's this," when someone brushed my arm. I turned to see the sweet smile of my *Clematis* devotee. Behind her stood a man, leaning ever so slightly above her as if that were his customary pose, her protector. In his hands, the *Clematis* his wife had so adored, looking radiant as did she.

"Hi. This is Robert, my husband." Her smile grew more luminous. "And my name is Mayleen."

Sowing Seeds of Royalty

I sat with the catalogue open on my lap, my back against the hemlock we called our magic tree, looking out through its sweeping limbs. Its branches climbed in wedding cake layers, reaching for the land of giants and kings. Royalty in the guise of *Tsuga caroliniana*, it promised favors, if only one would come closer, shelter beneath its spreading wings. Its magic as seductive as the spell being cast by the deceptively humble, Times New Roman printed pages I held in my hands – the Royal Horticultural Society's current free seeds listing. Recognizing only one out of every three offerings, still my pulse raced, my breathing becoming labored, my mouth watering. I tasted Neverland.

Being able to use the RHS member symbol on my brochures and business cards and newsletters would have been thrill enough. But a glossy botanical tome called The Plantsman had landed in the mailbox three times since I'd given myself, well, The Herb of Grace, an RHS Christmas present.

Now, eyes darting from one Latin name to another, I had gone from feeling slightly uppity about my membership to the hallowed halls of Kew to feeling lost and humbled in the presence of so many botanical splendors. What was a *Bellevalia*? Sitting on the floor surrounded by horticultural encyclopedias, magazines, catalogs, I discovered it's a genus of plants in the family *Asparagaceae*, subfamily *Scilloideae* and described as a genus in 1808. In the age of Google, I could have also found out that the approximately 65 species making up the genus can be found in the Mediterranean region: Turkey and Israel, to central Asia: Iran, Afghanistan and Pakistan. Or it's some type of game found on something called Twitch.

I ordered a *Bellevalia*, along with other botanicals I'd never encountered, like *Cerathotheca* (South African Foxglove) and some I had, like *Cistus* and *Codonopsis* (Rock Rose and a beautiful, tender vine).

Weeks, months would pass before the seeds arrived. So, after a day spent pulling weeds, I ordered taxonomic books. A day playing pie lady to a thirsty horde of plantaholics was followed by an evening tearing out those little blow-in cards, subscribing to Gardens Illustrated and English Garden. By the time I held the small manila mailer stamped "Royal Mail" in my hands, I felt slightly more informed. They knew me, those gardening Brits; they included a germination and cultivation guide. I still refer to its tattered, soil-grimed pages every spring and every fall.

I sat cross-legged on the grass, the earth breathing beneath me, exhaling the mists of a mountain morning. Monday and I felt like a little kid released to the freedom of summer of a school holiday, the whole day before me. Elbows on knees, I leaned over, looking at the rich dark soil enjoying its own freedom from cold and winter, basking in the sun, releasing its primordial scent of leaf mold and moss and long-dead trees.

Ignoring me and my human reveries, a wren piped from inside a 'Blue Billow' *Hydrangea*. Finishing his own musings, he hopped to the ground to peck at a bit of dandelion fluff, moved on. Unearthed by all the avian activity, a knuckle of slick purples and blues formed a little hump in the scattered soil. From my adulterated Yoga Fold, it looked like Adam emerging from the dust, fist raised to the heavens. I scratched around searching for a tag and discovered its migration to the back side of a Japanese maple. "*Crambe maritima* – RHS seed exchange."!

Paradise Lost

The same Magic Tree that greeted customers on their way up the walk to the shop, that called to me to come sit and find solace, or to order seeds from across the ocean, once hid a suddenly quiet three-year-old while his frantic mother cried and everyone else searched. This same regal hemlock that had sheltered Kim's new puppy, Andy, from the heat and protected a Brownie troop of elves from a downpour, one fateful day met Alfred.

Alfred played piano, substituting for the regulars at venues across the county. Michala sold gold chains, silver bracelets and diamond earrings at a store in the strip mall south of the city. During the lean times, Alfred landscaped for the neighbors, borrowing their lawnmowers and string trimmers. Michala sold baubles and thought positive thoughts, both chanting the mantra of positive thinking, "Name it and claim it." And this Alfred did. For what he truly longed to claim was his place upon this land. So he spread the word that he now designed landscapes. Michala only wanted Alfred happy, or at least not whining. Both compact and delicately made, they looked like the couple swinging in and out of a Tyrolean cuckoo clock, if the Tyrolean had met a nice Italian girl.

There were two ways to make an acquaintance in our valley – at the cafe or through Millie. She introduced us as "the people at The Herb of Grace place" and Alfred and Michala as "neighbors between me and you, live on a piece of land so steep the rocks need a flat ass to sit on."

Invited to dinner one night – lentil bean soup and bruschetta with fresh tomatoes – we stepped outside to survey their garden and Alfred's design work. Groupings of the said flat ass rocks climbed the hill, interspersed with sculptures created from recycled auto parts and surrounded by waves of a lovely lavender *Phlox*. Actually, it was rather charming in a positive thinking kind of way. So, I asked him if he'd contract to mow the grass at our house and shop. He sounded eager to start and only a little cagey when it came to telling me when I could expect him. And, oh yes, "How about a lawn mower?"

He arrived on a Tuesday, day two of my weekend, which suited me perfectly. Swooning from lack of proper attention, a grow house full of seedling *Geraniums* and *Campanulas* needed sustenance, a roomy new pot, fresh furnishings, and a dose of time-release fertilizer. And I being their handmaiden, showed Alfred the lawnmower, the gas can and left him to it.

Lost in thought, plants playing Zen master, a couple of hours passed before Alfred appeared at the door of the potting shed. Face beaming, he said he was finished and I should follow him. Like a cross between a preschooler and a Chihuahua, he bounced, skittering from the shed to the bridge, then across the garden, talking over his shoulder all the while. At the blue door, he did a little two-step and ushered me through ahead of him. I climbed the steps, entered the cool wash of air that lives, always, between smokehouse and springhouse. At the parking lot, I slowed. My feet dragged, then halted as I looked toward the shop.

As Alfred rattled on about his concept, I said nothing. The sight before me struck me dumb, rendering any response impossible. I just prayed it would strike me blind as well. I finally managed to turn my head and look at Alfred pointing with his Paul Bunyan loppers toward my precious, my sacred Magic Tree. To a height of twelve feet (he must have found a ladder somewhere), he had pruned all branches from the hemlock's majestic trunk, leaving it naked and exposed, all its drama, its hermitage, its solace, its magic stripped away on a Tuesday afternoon. Alfred had, thoughtfully, stacked the dying branches in a neat, somewhat sculptural pile.

Countryside Trails and Farm Tours

A crow flying from our valley to either of our two towns big enough for a legitimate grocer runs around eight or nine miles. By road, say, fourteen, fifteen. To make it in the car seldom took under an hour, which according to John, was way too much thinking time for me. Those long, looping miles helped hatch up some of my more imaginative (not to say lucrative) marketing schemes: Talk and Takeaway for an NPR fundraiser, Revolving Garden Club promotion days, Show and Tells at the AG center, herb displays at welcome centers, classes in concocting rose water and brewing herb vinegars, propagating perennials and weaving lavender wands, and, of course, the infamous Spring Galas and Fall Festivals.

If a small business in the middle of nowhere has any chance of even buying a coffer, much less filling it, the owner will spend more time whipping those dogs and ponies into fine, show-stopping shape than she does anything else. It's a lot of work, a lot of creative wool gathering. But once in a blue moon, opportunity doesn't have to be wooed. It comes looking for you.

In 1995, a group of North Carolinians gathered to talk about the state's beautiful mountains and the good people who lived along their ridges, in their coves and valleys and small towns. And from that gathering, the organization HandMade in America was founded. In their own words taken from their Farms, Gardens & Countryside Trails of Western North Carolina Guidebook, the second of two guidebooks, the first being The Craft Heritage Trails, funded by grants from a number of North Carolina Commissions and Initiatives, it embodied "an organization dedicated to the nurturance of craft culture and community." Included in both, an entry for Herb of Grace Farm (close enough) pictured our blue door welcoming in another wave of travelers eager for meaning in their journeys, their destinations.

These guidebooks, along with Kim's seasonal press releases, provided the best kind of advertising, the kind you don't have to pay for.

All of it bore fruit. In the case of the Trail books, they sprouted another growing initiative, the Farm Tours, usually scheduled on a Sunday in August, said day either steaming under storm clouds or parched by drought. Our first tour dawned with the mountain version of a sirocco, dust-laden winds that swooped through the nursery and across the Verandah at Formula 1 speeds. Hard to make a floral presentation atop a silver tier for tea with the tablecloths whipping bare legs to a blistering windburn. But the tables were full, and the crowds heaved with curiosity.

Did I not have iced tea? I did. This one I'd anticipated, down to the paper cups so they could carry them out to the barn where John was on standby with Josie, Spencer, and assorted Angoras. In the garden, Ruby kept an eye out for possible chicken interest. I manned the refreshment station, which is what the shop came to be that day.

I found out farm tours beguiled families, couples in need of a reason for a Sunday drive, and congregants from the latest back-to-the-land movement. The first needed somewhere for the kids to run off some of that energy – barn, hen house, goat hill. The second needed a restroom break and the third wanted to absorb the ambiance and check out the plant tables. Offerings of culinary herbs did little to assuage their hunger for the big three – ginseng, goldenseal and jewelweed. I felt like an imposter with my French soaps and lovely roses. Cinderella to the wildly popular stepsisters, the shop was needed only as a way station on the way to livelier pursuits. I went to bed that night with the blood-curdling screams of marauding children still playing in my head.

Better prepared the second time the tour came our way, we set up a dispenser for iced tea and cold water and sold our blue and brown eggs out of the kitchen door and raw Angora hair in bags set in a French laundry basket. We no longer expected our meager sales to do more than shave the top off the expense for ice tea and Ruby's wages. I no longer expected to see any of them again, and in this, I proved to be prophetic. But the tourists always seemed to be having a great time, and we consoled ourselves with being good citizens to our fellow travelers. But we did harvest a couple of offshoots from our inclusion in the Farm Tours.

Late July, on a day foggy with gnats and No-See-Ums, Roger stuck his head in the door I'd just unlatched. He was cradling a flat of frail and listless green things. I knew Roger from the Growers Association meetings, but I'd done no more than nod at him, usually from the fringes of a crowd he'd cornered for his bio-diverse sermons. In his rarified sphere, I always felt intimidated, an idiot wandering in by accident. This man took his role as herbal arbiter seriously, and one slunk meekly from his presence, humbled. Or so it seemed.

Draped in a scarecrow's khakis on that day, he ducked inside, knuckled his glasses up his nose and said, "I hope you don't mind, but I wondered if you'd take a couple of flats of goldenseal, maybe one of ginseng to sell during the Farm Tour. I'm not set up for the public and I'd really appreciate it."

I sold them all in the first half-hour. When he stopped by later to pick up his money, he brought a few more flats at my request. He proved to be a good and steady friend, not a lot of socializing, but I always felt him there in my corner. Years later, he delivered a condolence card, took my hand, and told me he'd been a little afraid of me when we first met. "But you weren't nearly as uppity as you looked."

Introduction to Tim was more straightforward. A young, newly-appointed extension agent, he helped organize and led the first Farm Tour. Often out our way, he liked to stop by for a cup of Earl Grey and a visit. His family grew flue-cured tobacco further east, and he had an affinity for the mountain farmers, with their quarter-acre patches squeezed between ridges. A farm of a hundred acres might provide only an acre or two of tillable ground. Tobacco was the only crop they knew, paying enough to put shoes on the feet of their children.

"But tobacco causes lung cancer and the little farmer is the sacrificial scapegoat for the industry." A gentle young man, Tim's voice always took on a spurt of anger at this point. He sat up straighter in his chair, leaned in to his argument. "And nobody cares. Not the anti-tobacco protester and certainly not the big tobacco companies. After all, there are a lot of smokers still. Across the water. And that doesn't seem to bother the sanctimonious."

A sermonizer as well, Tim preached innovation, new ways of farming, new crops, and the marketing of those crops, his congregation the deep valley farmers. But the road forward was a hard one, tobacco being all most of these farmers knew for generations. That and a few cows steady enough on their feet not to tip over on the steep ridges.

I think he saw The Herb of Grace and me as a small part of the possibilities for some kind of solution. At one point, he asked if I'd be one of the speakers at the community college on diversifying the farm. I enjoyed that day, felt well-received, and I so appreciated it. I had my doubts about changing any minds or ways of living. It seemed a daunting, impossible task. But change did begin, slowly, new ideas as a way to keep the farms, the families together in these mountains.

Connections and friends and customers resulted from these two gentlemen; along with the eggs and bags of goat hair sold, not a bad return from the Farm Tours.

Farther Afield

Thieves Among the Revelers

Purloined goods were never a problem for us at the Herb Festivals or the Plant Faires, even when the crowds juggled each other for foot space, and I couldn't see our wares two feet left of center, much less to the parking lot thirty feet in the distance. I never gave thievery a thought until the year of the hellebores.

Back in the mid 1990s, hellebores (*Helleborus x hybridus*) were just beginning the shift from the back pages of the gardening magazines, where I'd fallen in love with a pastel line drawing and the words "winter bloom" to article status. Plant breeders in the UK and Germany, the Pacific Northwest and our own South had begun crossing the *Helleborus orientalis* with other species, creating magical blooms in elegant colors and shapes.

On a trip back from a spring visit to my parents in North Florida, I took the back roads across central Georgia, stopping at yard sales, antique stores, and "Plants for Sale" signs. South of Athens, I saw a sign swirling with balloons covering everything except the word "...plants" and an arrow pointing east. I swung right. As I bumped up the gravel road, dodging rain-gouged ruts, I realized something special must be going on. Cars were parked bumper to tailpipe all along the piney woods bordering the drive. I backed up and then pulled over to my own patch of pines.

People milled about among the trees as if lost in paradise. As my eyes adjusted, I saw a haze of ivory, a smoke of purple. A blustery February day and blooms covered the earth. I'd happened upon Hellebore Days at Piccadilly Farms, owned by professor emeritus at the University of Georgia Athens, Samuel A. Jones, Jr. and his wife, Carleen. I recognized the names from the little ad I'd seen in the back pages of my garden magazine. I brought a dozen hellebores back to the gardens and began to scout out a liner source for nursery stock.

Before the birth of the Internet, networking meant trade shows, magazines, the telephone. Calling state and national plant associations for lists of their members took days, weeks before I held the membership books in my hands. The Southeastern Nurserymen's Association members filled two fat green and white volumes, among them Pine Knot Farms in Clarksville, Virginia. I ordered the liners and began a long relationship with two preeminent Hellebore breeders – Dick and Judith Tyler of Pine Knot Farms.

Now grown up and living in gallons, those liner babies were looking good and causing a stir. The only vendor that year at the Herb Festival to carry hellebores, we had staged them in an old wooden wheelbarrow at the front of the booth.

I noticed the woman as she shoved her way through the crowd, parting the other shoppers like Moses with his Red

Sea, her rod a one-gallon hellebore, its blooms a dusky blue the color of slate-paved forest floor. She shook it at me.

"Ten-fifty. That's ridiculous. I'll pay six dollars."

"I'm sorry. Ten-Fifty."

"You won't get that."

"I've been getting it all day."

"Eight."

"Sorry." And hoping to discourage the haggling, I turned away to another customer peering under a table at a row of lady ferns.

A few minutes later, I made the rounds, checking for thirsty plants. I reached the wheelbarrow of hellebores and bent to poke my finger in the soil, testing. I smiled at the holes left in the display by happy hunters and began rearranging pots – white picotee next to a pale pink speckled raspberry, next to... My hand hovered above the cavity, empty except for a smattering of soil. I glanced around to be sure. Nope. My beautiful blue was missing.

I wished for bad karma. I cast a spell for an unhappy association. I stopped short of hoping it died on her.

Arriving home at dusk, turning in our gate with its closed sign dangling, shutting it behind us, we climbed out of the car, taking with us only the empty Big Mac and fries' bag. Time enough tomorrow to unload. We drug ourselves down the stone steps leading to the nursery tables. Water needs trumped our aching bodies. Weighted down by one of our two dollar and fifty cents, 4-inch 'Pink Chintz' thymes, we found a dollar bill, two quarters and a folded piece of tablet paper. The penciled note read, "Sorry we missed you. We bought a flat of your lavenders. Thanks."

We walked back up the steps and locked the car.

Feeding the Soul on Hyacinths and Irony

I'd gotten used to people at the festivals; their faces crinkled into excited smiles, approaching every plant as if it were the treasure they'd lost in the secret garden of childhood. But few could equal the tiny woman, clad in purple overalls, who laughed and gleamed and oohed over every flower she sniffed and touched. In her wake, everyone's grins broadened, suddenly happier as if anointed by Tinkerbell's wand. By the time she reached us at the back of the booth, her arms sagged with pots of gillyflower, harebells, and lavender.

Bullying along behind, trying to catch up, a man dressed up in a brown, Sunday go-to-meeting suit, thundered, "By God, Liu, that's enough."

Trying to soothe the troubled waters, Pollyanna me smiled at them both. I said, "But hyacinths feed the soul."

He stopped. Glared. Snorted. Then drew himself to his full righteous height. Oozing scorn, he spat, "I'll have you know, Missy, only God feeds my soul."

It was the seventh day in the Garden and God smiled in the irony of sunshine and Eden.

Gracious Me! It's Southern Living!

The first weekend in May and Mother's Day on the horizon – sweet words to a winter-poor cavalcade of Herb Festival vendors. Sending its minions further south to drench middle Georgia and bluster northern Alabama, the weather smiled on Western North Carolina, and we felt like favored children.

Excited crowds snatched bronze fennel, Corsican mint, St. John's wort off the truck before we'd set the brake. Grabbing moss roses, bourbon, noisettes out of our hands and off the back of the truck as we struggled with our tables and wares. Like intercity gangs, gardeners shoved, cursed and flailed to get at a particularly fetching group of scented geraniums. Hungering with their voracious botanical appetites, I think we could have slapped a label on a pot of dandelions and sold it to the congregants as a "lovely, sunny groundcover." And judging from the dazed expressions and the disbelieving grins I saw, it seemed all our neighboring plant purveyors suffered from the same glorious malady.

By noon, the crowd, a beleaguered bunch, had gathered down at the food concession, swatting at wasps, waiting their turns for a burrito and latte. John, back from the nursery with another load, dumped trays of herbs and perennials and scented geraniums onto the tables and a hodgepodge of roses down onto the asphalt. The afternoon settled into a soothing rhythm of buying, selling, replenishing.

Mouth stretched wide in a tooth revealing yawn, I was anticipating a bucket of chicken and a cessation of trade when she walked up, still looking like 8 a.m. on a spring morning, holding a 'Lemon Crispum' scented geranium.

"Hello." Her accent of cream-whipped sorghum identified her as a home-grown Georgia Peach.

"Do you need a bag?" I asked and pointed to the *Pelargonium*.

"No. Well, yes, but are you Bobbie? I'm Ellen Riley, Associate Garden Editor for *Southern Living* Magazine."

I felt like I did when elected Halloween queen in sixth grade. As if somewhere a catch awaited the unsuspecting and the gullible. While its parent magazine, The Progressive Farmer had provided generations of my family tree with everything necessary for "the betterment of farm life," its offspring, *Southern Living*, presented us our Christmas cakes. Now on this hallowed day, Ellen wanted our scented geraniums to star in an upcoming issue, their photo shoot to take place where they grew up – The Herb of Grace. I imagined my grandmothers beaming with pride. I'd amounted to something after all.

In anticipation of the *Southern Living* article, we grew an excess of scented geraniums that year. I got carried away. Too tired at the end of the day to fall asleep, I'd lay awake, watching out the window as night revealed its inhabitants, an owl hooting from the barn, a groundhog snuffling through the brush, as thoughts circled without mercy, round and round like a Bradbury carrousel, spooky and malicious. Morning brought optimism, birds chirping portents and possibilities, sun shining promises, and I'd go out to the propagation house and harvest more cuttings for yet more scented geraniums. Too bad I failed to lasso a few of those circling thoughts and use them for a little rational thinking.

By the end of summer, the geraniums – hanging from every rafter; perched on every wall, lining every pathway – sagged under their own leafy weight. A Monday in late August on the habitual run from shop to nursery, we lopped their branches and gathered them into bed-sheets. Duffy chugged along with me, stopping on the backside of the old smokehouse to roll in the doggy delight of a days-old, unidentifiable, pathetically dead mammal. Afterward, he stretched out in the sun, down-wind from my pruning. I grabbed his collar and a handful of geranium branches and gave him a good scrub. The day continued much improved.

For months I used fresh then dry rose, nutmeg, lemon, chocolate scented and smooth, rough, crimped, crinkled, variegated leaves as dog brushes, cat combs, instant potpourri under chair cushions, in closets, in the chicken house for nesting material. A customer bought a bundle off the shop door, and I did a brisk business in geranium leaf swags for a week or so. The plants themselves looked like stick figures, embarrassed, shorn of their vanities. But in days they began to preen in tiny new leaves

In those few months leading up to *Southern Living*'s visit, we hustled. Ruby appointed herself garden director, chivvying our two summer volunteers when it looked like they were having more fun than they ought. Even the plants flushed green and lush, as if afraid Ruby might start on them next. Every moment Kim could spare from her own business, she spruced the shop, rearranging displays, buying a menu board and easel for the Verandah. With a flourish, she wrote, "Today's Tea: Passion Flower." We felt quite recherché.

Shortly before Ellen arrived with a photographer and assistant, she called to interview me about the care and propagation of fragrant *Pelargoniums.*

Thinking back to my first encounter with a scented geranium, I remembered she sat in a fat and happy crowd of rosemaries, like a lost, precocious child in a frilly petticoat. Intending to find the rest of her family somewhere on those nursery tables, I picked her up and stroked the soft green of her small fan shaped leaves. Like my favorite childhood candy, they smelled of coconut.

Intrigued by this first introduction to the scented leaf siblings of the hot-house bedding geranium, I sought out a source for other scents of this member in the genus *Pelargonium.*

They proved to be a propagator's dream, rooting easily. Their South African lineage makes them a pot plant in Zone 8 and colder. They can live inside over the winter, looking a little anorexic before spring arrives to prod them out of their doldrums. One year, Kim's 'Attar of Roses' in its winter home of a west-facing window lost all of its leaves save two at the tip of its tallest branch. A drape of shiny red beads saw it through Christmas.

I told Ellen some of this during our phone call and about our favorite varieties.

The Day. A sunrise promising perfection. But Ellen and the young lady assisting the photographer, Ralph Anderson, carried chairs, shifted tables, and staged pots of those saucy geraniums in the worst heat of the summer. Every gnat residing in the vicinity of the creek jollied up to watch the goings on. But the gardens, the shop, they did look grand.

We poured the *Southern Living* crew cup after cup of tea, supplied them with constant bottles of water and attempted to help without getting in the way. At the end of the day, when I tried to tell them how nice, how kind they'd been, how much I appreciated the opportunity and their work and their magazine, they thanked us.

The article appeared in the June issue, almost a year after Ellen Riley came to the fair. She turned my words into gems of wisdom and presented our scented geraniums like debutantes at the cotillion. In the main picture, The Herb of Grace blue door served as backdrop to a lovely ensemble of *Pelargonium* performers. Another picture and Kim's thumb became a star as she stroked the cupped leaf of an 'Attar of Roses.'

260

Unlocking the door, my hands full of invoices, I walked into the shop and knew our issue of *Southern Living* had landed in mailboxes across the South and beyond. Fourteen and counting, the number of flashes on the answering machine, and the phone calls continued, unabated, for weeks from all over the country. From people frantic for scented geraniums – by post. Which we were not set up to provide. We referred a lot of callers to Sandy Mush Herb Nursery that summer. After a few months, their thank yous became a bit strained.

But our benefits from association with the iconic *Southern Living* proved more lasting than a summer fling. Years later, customers were still poking their heads in our door, asking for scented geraniums and staying for tea.

Some of our Favorite Scented Geraniums

'Old Fashioned Rose'

'Attar of Roses'   'Both's Snowflake'

Snow Flurry'   'Joy Lucille'

'Chocolate Mint'   'Cinnamon Rose'

'Lavender Lady'   'Lemon   Meringue

'Lemon Crispum'   'Velvet-Rose'

'Fringed Apple'   'Wynchwood Rose'

'Angel'   'Nutmeg'

'Old Spice'

'Lady Mary'

'Coconut'

A Merchant and a Samaritan on their Way to an Inn...

Highland Lake Inn in Flat Rock, North Carolina, was built as a private home in 1845 and named "Solitude." It shed many identities, lodged its share of famous people (Joanne Woodward) and harbored its share of spirits on its way to being Historic.

Over the years, stone cottages and clapboard bungalows joined the original mansion, the forest of hemlocks, oaks, and laurels retaking the disturbed land until the buildings looked like nature-crafted puzzle pieces in the wooded landscape. It seemed removed from a world of chaos, offering those retreating there respite from their everyday lives.

And on a fine day in May, it was offering to the interested a horticultural society-sponsored symposium. Scheduled to talk about the highs and lows of running a nursery and retail shop, I jostled alongside my fellow speakers to the Inn's main dining room to partake of a lunch of fresh greens and tomatoes, local cheese and artisan bread; then turned loose to roam the two-acre organic vegetable and herb garden behind the Inn. It lacked a historic wall and a parterre, but the long rows did step pleasantly down the hillside toward the lake.

In a row dedicated to tomatoes, I saw my first tomatillo and a purple basil with a licorice flavor I later learned belonged to the variety 'Rubin.' I'm ashamed to admit I felt a twinge of satisfaction when, even in this iconic garden, I saw knotgrass sneaking into the row of thymes.

Directed to a conference room overlooking the lake, I stepped in to see every chair occupied, jiggling beneath the posteriors of eager acolytes. They all wanted a piece of the dream.

My notes never made it out of my pocket, my lecture hijacked by forty-five minutes of Q & A.

"How much start-up money do you need?"

"More." I heard tittering from the back row.

"Excuse me?"

"You'll always need more than you think."

"How many hours do you work?"

"Twelve. Except when we have a large lunch crowd scheduled, then it's fourteen, maybe fifteen. And, oh yeah, in spring, it's more like sixteen hours, because I have to be in the potting shed by six and in the garden after closing time til dark."

"A day?"

"Yes."

The chairs had stopped jiggling. I had not so much lost my audience as stunned them speechless.

"Okay. Right. It is true I've never worked harder in my life, and it's also true I'm the last one to get a paycheck, and it's usually rather pitiful." The chairs were on the move again.

"Wait. But it's true, too, that not for one minute, of even one of those sixteen-hour days in all the years I've been working them, have I ever been bored. And I still wake up every morning feeling like a little girl getting up to go outside into the sunshine and play make-believe."

I now heard the sound of chairs shifting a little and saw a fair number of smiles ripple through the room. I even saw a few stars glisten again in a few eyes. But the most heart-felt thank you I received that day came from a slender brunette with a beautiful creamy complexion – untouched by either blistering sun or raging wind – and a killer manicure.

"Thank you. Really. You've saved me from one disastrous mistake."

Tearoom & Shop

British Meets American

Just inside and to the right of our tall entrance doors, large glass jars, labeled and filled with the treasures of the Orient, sat atop a once dilapidated sideboard - rescued, painted purple, and covered in silvery metal flashing. Its drawers accommodated our tea reserves. We bagged tea straight from these jars, scooping and filling the offerings of the day. On the shelves of a display wall built of corrugated tin, teapots, tea cozies, and tea infusers jostled together in a bid for new converts to the realm of taking tea. Behind the wall in the kitchen, the smell of baking croissants, scones and tarts mingled with the fragrance of freshly brewed tea.

During the winter of our great building adventure, it hit me. An actual tearoom would become a permanent, everyday part of our family. The brochures would read "The Herb of Grace - Shop, Gardens, Nursery, and Tearoom," and I could no longer make do with Sam's Club Earl Grey. I went on the hunt for real tea.

The British American Tea Company was another of Victoria's "Favorite Things." My phone call reached a business only a few hours away in Durham, North Carolina, and the voice on the other end sounded like a chipper Sean

Connery. A lovely man with his plummy vowels, he tantalized with his suggestions, tempted with his recommendations from exotic lands.

"An Oolong, perhaps. Also, a Sri Lankan, small leaf, I think. China black, Assam, Darjeeling. Now that I think about it, we might need to add a few flavors to the black and a Green, something like our Island Peach Coconut."

By guiding me through his offerings, reeling me back in when my kid in a candy store enthusiasm threatened to swamp me in tea, he became co-creator of the Verandah.

It varied over the years. Island Peach Coconut giving way to Black Currant during our autumn season. Royal Gunpowder introduced as a mysterious newcomer, lingered as an old friend. We remained faithful to the British American Tea Company, never straying as other sources offered discounts and specials. Even though we started not knowing a Nepal Ilam from a Vietnam Black, Reginald treated us like partners, and in doing so, educated us, banishing our ignorance. The Herb of Grace family loved our tea. For Kim it was a toss-up between a Darjeeling and smoky Royal Gunpowder. For me, nothing ever soothed like an Oolong. Maree preferred a Tropical Green; Ruby loved the "one with the strawberries in it." John was the exception. He preferred a good strong cup of Eight O'Clock coffee.

Of Perils and Pitfalls

Born of serendipitous happenstance, Tea at The Herb of Grace stumbled its way through our first years only to find its role as leading lady at the new shop, drawing in the crowds to be seduced (I hoped) by my first loves - the nursery, the gardens and the shop.

Although the Verandah's popularity grew beyond anyone's expectations, the simple kitchen I walked into every dawn never progressed beyond the bare basics. I steamed tomato wine soup on a family stove, baked the tarts in its single oven. As temperamental as an artiste or a toddler, my oven fluctuated, somewhat like the houses of the three little pigs, from too hot to too cool to just right - every morning a gamble. With the building of the shop, we installed a dishwasher and stainless counter in a tiny prep kitchen hidden behind waves of shiny metal wall. But the real kitchen, five hundred steps to the west, still served to whip up our suppers after its day job for the tearoom.

Ask any chef, disasters occur in the best of kitchens, and our old-fashioned cook's kitchen and minute-regulation prep kitchen, along with our location miles from anything resembling a farmer's market or grocery store, served up some doozies.

I awoke to the smell of rain through the half-open window. But weather being as changeable as my fortunes at that time of year, I paid it little mind, rising to a day filled with opportunity for good or ill – back-to-back reservations on the Verandah.

Plugging in the percolator, I laid out the butter, cream cheese, and eggs for teacakes and lemon bars. The third sweet, Double Chocolate Gateau, sat on the table under a robin-bedecked tea towel, mellowing from the day before. Since I'd prepared the teacakes a thousand times and the bars used a short-cut pound cake mix, I'd be able to coast through the morning. To clear the oven for the longer-baking bars, I twisted the knob to 350 degrees and watched for the red light to go off. I think.

There's something to be said for being in the zone, but something else altogether to be on autopilot. Two batches of bread, an array of quiches, an assortment of pâté, savories, cheeses fruits, and pastries later, I was ready, and ahead of schedule. I put the kettle on a low boil, the savories in the warmer, and opened the shop doors.

I'd been swapping some plant tales with a Clematis customer and enjoying it, thoroughly, when the first tea reservation arrived. Handing off my customer to a reluctant Ruby, I made my apologies and hustled to the kitchen. Kim, between cropping pictures and laying out a brochure, had come over to rescue Mom from another episode in the life of an overbooked shopkeeper. Now, she stood over the lemon squares, knife frozen as something that looked a lot like days-old egg yolk blossomed around the blade.

I dipped my finger in the golden ooze and tasted it, essence of lemon grove under the Tuscan sun, but with the consistency of a runny mousse or, maybe, a jar of Gerber's banana pudding. I checked the teacakes, broke off a piece and munched, breathed relief. Perfect bake.

"Can you stall?"

Kim grabbed bags of Japanese Rose Garden, Darjeeling, and Royal Gunpowder teas, placed them on a tray and hit the Verandah with a production (worthy of Lerner and Loewe) on the olfactory merits of each tea. What a kid.

While Kim was out front, waving a hand over a bag, offering a whiff, I rummaged through the refrigerator and found the cream cheese and sour cream hiding behind the butter. Paired with a mere thought of blueberries and a quick blend, it bore a resemblance to Devonshire cream. Then I scooped and dumped the failed lemon bars into stemmed glass compotes and spooned my faux clotted cream over the top, slicing through a couple of times with a bread knife. The unsweetened cream mellowed the mouth-puckering sweetness of the lemon concoction, and the tea guests moaned in pleasure. The dish became a favorite. Desperation makes top chefs of us all.

Mousse au Citron

First Layer:

    One box pound cake mix

    One egg

    One stick butter, melted

    Second Layer

    Two Eggs

    One (8-oz) package cream cheese

    Two tablespoons lemon thyme

    One teaspoon lemon juice

    One box confectioners' sugar

Clotted Cream (so called)

    One (8-oz) package cream cheese

    One (8-oz) carton sour cream

    ¼ cup fresh blueberries.Process until smooth.

Preheat oven to 350 degrees.

Mix layers one and two separately. Oil and flour an 11 x 13 inch pan. Spread layer one in the pan then spread layer two on top.

Bake to a jiggly consistency, about 30 minutes. Top with clotted cream (so called) and slice through a few times with a knife, marbling the mousse, or pudding, or confection a la crème, or making lemonade out of lemons.

Not yet over, the day had been a good one, though long and tiring. In the mix with buying supplies for the Verandah, banking deposits and shopping for groceries, Kim and I had picked up her young cat, Mimi, from the spay and neuter clinic in Woodfin.

We'd met Mimi a few weeks earlier when we pulled in the drive of Kim's latest rental house — another old farmhouse — the only affordable thing to be had on the creek after her cabin burned to the ground. Waiting on the front porch as if to welcome Kim home, a half-grown kitten, blinked and walked in the door on dainty sable paws, turning once to see if we had sense enough to follow. We found out later from the neighbors that she had been sitting like that for months, waiting for the family who abandoned her in the middle of the night, refusing to believe such treachery. From the doorway, she looked at Kim and yowled as if to say, "You'll do."

Six miles into our homeward journey, I tapped Kim on the knee and nodded toward the back seat. Inside her crate, Mimi rolled and tumbled, purring as if enraptured at her liberation from one tomcat or another. And thanked us from the bottom of her feline heart.

After dropping Kim and Mimi off, I drove back up the road and pulled into the back drive to unload bags and boxes. Glancing up the hill behind the barn, counting goats, locating Josie mid-flock, it hit me. I'd forgotten to buy the dark chocolate for tomorrow's tearoom torte. My shoulders slumped, every muscle aching with the thought of crawling back in the car, heading back over the mountain, driving the forty-five-minute challenge of curves and switchbacks to an overly-crowded grocery store, and back again, for a single pound of chocolate. Even the two miles further on to the store at the creek, where they might or might not have what I needed, seemed beyond me.

Stirring up a dust cloud in my tango of indecision, I shuffled toward the hatchback, then the door, then back again. Taking pity, the fates stirred a memory of a Brownie troop meeting in a far off sun-filled land on a gossipy, wind-whipped day and the gift of an old-fashioned chocolate/chocolate cake and its recipe. My cupboard held a surfeit of cocoa; no need to go anywhere but inside. But if you've built a French farmhouse-style shop with wide Verandah, you can't call it a cake or chocolate/chocolate, so I called the crew together, and after a number of eye-rolls, we ended up with this:

Double Chocolate Gateau
Cake:
   One cup butter
   One cup water
   Two cups flour
   Two cups granulated sugar
   Four tablespoons powdered cocoa
   One teaspoon baking soda
   ¼ teaspoon salt
   ½ cup buttermilk
   Two eggs
   One teaspoon vanilla extract
Preheat oven to 350 degrees.

Melt butter and a cup of water in a large saucepan. Remove from heat. In a large bowl, sift together flour, sugar, cocoa, baking soda and salt. Add to saucepan. Beat on low with a portable mixer. Add buttermilk, eggs, and vanilla. Beat until smooth. Pour into a 15 ½ x 9-inch pan. Bake for 30 minutes.

Meanwhile prepare Frosting:
   One stick butter
   Four tablespoons milk
   One teaspoon vanilla extract
   One box confectioners' sugar and Three tablespoons cocoa

Melt butter with milk and add vanilla. Sift in cocoa and sugar. Beat until smooth and pour over cake while still hot.

We topped it with crème fraiche and a few fresh raspberries. Through the years, we varied toppings: toasted pecans or almonds or cherries or shredded coconut or rose petals. Once I spread a layer of chunky peanut butter over the still hot cake and then poured the frosting over it. The gateau in all its guises became a staple.

A glut of springtime eggs sparked our Egg Caviar (Yes, I know I could have named it simply egg salad.)

Egg Caviar

Six hard-boiled eggs, chopped

¼ cup Duke's mayonnaise

Two teaspoons Dijon mustard

½ teaspoon ground curry

Two tablespoon fresh chopped chives

One teaspoon fresh tarragon, chopped

One teaspoon balsamic vinegar

Salt & freshly ground pepper to taste

Place all ingredients in a food processor and pulse until consistency of a slightly lumpy spread.

Serve with rosemary-infused toasted French bread. Infusion: olive oil, balsamic vinegar, and a sprig of rosemary.

Kim or I would go out into the garden, early morning, long before the shop opened. Dew still silvering the herbs, we harvested for this dish – a snip of thyme, a few leaves of marjoram, or a snip of winter savory. Whatever appealed to us at day's beginning.

Once Upon a Royal Visit

What do you do when you're expecting The (capital T) Garden Club, the nurseryman's dream of repeat customer and disposable income? And what if it's rained for six days straight and the grass and the weeds in the garden look like marauding hordes and your beautiful roses and perennials look like a village of sodden wenches, resigned to their fate? And it's ten minutes 'til show-time.

I cleared the gate between our private domain and the garden's public face with a plan in hand (sleight of hand), a little hocus pocus, a bit of staging. Choreographing a weaving pattern worthy of a professional tight-end, I snapped the heads off spent blooms; snagged strands of bindweed; dumped rocks – artistically – into the hole left by the 6-foot tall clump of Johnson grass we'd somehow missed in a border of *Dianthus* 'Bath's Pink,' that I finally see and pull in that last five minutes; all the while sweeping, with clog shod feet, gravel back onto pathways, mulch into beds. By the time I reached the rock wall separating the springhouse from the parking lot, I was staggering under the burden of foliage, soil, various plant pots, and a dead frog. I slowed just long enough to dump it all behind the boulder that anchored the rock wall surrounding the parking lot, hiding it behind a stalwart poplar.

Kicking off my shoes, aiming for a hidden corner of the courtyard, I hustled across the shop. Holding my hands above my head like a backwoods Flamenco dancer, I tried to prevent the detritus up my sleeves and under my fingernails from falling to the nice, clean floor – the floor scrubbed by my child 'til the wee hours of the night before, after her own long day of work. Once inside the restroom, I turned on the faucet, scoured my hands, ripped off the apron I'd been wearing to protect my clothes, and tossed it out the window to fall between the wall and the rising bank. I rinsed the sink, tucked back a stray hair, retrieved my inside shoes and stepped out to greet customers on the stroke of ten.

By noon the Verandah teemed with garden club members and a drive-by couple planning to infiltrate the gathering for free food. Disposing of the couple – inside on a loveseat with a cup and a cookie – I stepped back outside to find the club's president, vice-president, and three presidents emeritus trying to fit around a head table meant for four. Like a gang of musical chair- straddling preschoolers, they began nudging, then shoving, setting party hats atremble.

Before they could begin to square off – preschoolers morphing into goalies – Zee, home on college break, glided forward, smiled deferentially and slid another table next to the one under siege. With a flourish, she floated a white damask tablecloth, fragrant with lavender, over the two, creating unity where there had been division, calm where there had been chaos.

Commandeered for the day, our friend Babs all but curtsied and began pouring tea, "Royal Gunpowder or Irish Afternoon?" She started with the head table.

Two days of preparation – of cleaning, of polishing, of assembling, then sifting, kneading, chopping, sautéing – brought us to the telling hour. In tandem accompanied by the strings of Sibelius, Zee and Babs served the silver tiers, rich with the bounty of strawberries stacked in their juices, pods of green grapes blooming with crispness, a sprinkling of just-picked blueberries (snagged on that morning's hustle) all surrounding delicate triangles of Gouda, Brie, and Edam. Drifts of *Viola tricolor* adorned the cheeses. On the tier below, egg-rich quiche bubbled with spinach and mushrooms, and cups of tomato wine soup, garnished with parsley and thyme, steamed. Upon the bottom tier sat everyone's secret lust – slivers of almond rich tart, squares of double chocolate gateau and mounds of rose-water teacakes. The servers returned to place a trio of crystal pots on each table, filled with clotted cream, strawberry jam and lemon curd. Woven baskets awaited French bread.

Meanwhile, in the kitchen, two teakettles simmered. At the prep table, I sliced baguettes, smearing them with Boursin. A scow for buttery knives, caramelized sauté pans, clotted whisks, the sink refused to drain; the trash can erupted in discarded cling film, ripped parchment paper, empty cartons.

The floor resembled a modernist installation, all squished strawberries and oil-slick crumbs.

Outside on the Verandah, a tide of murmurs rose and fell, sailing on slurps of tea. Zee opened the top of the right-hand café door, blocking the view of the diners, leaving the other side closed as instructed. An "Employees Only" sign, mounted on both doors and, for good measure, on the wall, instructed patrons.

"More bread." From the head table, someone was talking with her mouth full. "And Boursin."

Back in the kitchen, Zee said, "Table four wants to know if there's more quiche?"

I've learned, so I answered, "No." Next it would be table five, then table two, then all of them clamoring like children for their sweeties. I would run out before everyone got their extras, and then I'd have tantrums. I sent out more bread.

By that time, I'd shanghaied Ruby from her beloved gardens and put her to washing up. Zee began to clear, swinging through the door, snagging it closed with a foot, dumping plates and tiers. Just as Babs grabbed the broom to shovel a path through the fruit salad on the floor, a meaty hand grabbed the café door, knuckles white, and with a swing to equal the Babe, flung it wide to a resounding thwack against the stucco wall. One of the presidents of emeritus status stood there looking in, drawn to full height and glory, eyes darting to and fro. Beneath her feet, a fallen sign read, "...oyees Only."

Inside the kitchen, Ruby froze, her hands immersed in a volcano of liver-colored suds. Babs, stooping to wield the

283

dustpan, stilled, caught with posterior skyward, and Zee dropped a cup, its shards mingling with a bitten kiwi slice, Klimpt like. And I choked on the teacake I'd just shoved in my mouth.

La president tilted back her head, flared her nostrils, a whiff of victory in her smirk. "We are out of Sugar!"

We scurried to prepare fresh tea for the next round.

I'm not sure which eminence was actually slated to present the program, but it ended up a chorus, a cacophony lasting sixty long minutes. After a mutiny of stifled yawns and whispered dissent among the constituency, the talk ground to a halt. And, "Questions anyone?" triggered a stampede into the shop and out to the plant benches.

I spent a happy hour outside under a June sky, talking pruning, fertilizing, roses and *Camellias*. Channeling Tom Sawyer, I had a group weeding ground ivy from pots of chamomile and deadheading *Dicentras* and *Veronicas* as we talked about Gertrude Jekyll and Beth Chatto and the loss of a well-made spade.

"Will you take us through the garden?" Graced by a summer afternoon, collecting other members along the way, we made for the garden gate. They were a lovely bunch, standing just beyond the blue door, grazing among the blueberry bushes. There may not have been enough quiche to satisfy their lunchtime hunger, but there was an abundance of blueberries.

Where 'Elsa Spath' wove her tendrils through 'Blush Noisette' – a seduction of tea rose and *Clematis* in an explosion of purple bloom and blush petal – Duffy joined us. Sauntering through a garden in the company of a Golden Retriever enveloped us in a Zen-like calm. In the shade garden, we stooped, sat, hunkered and knelt, each of us hearing the call of a kindred plant, a hellebore, a *Hydrangea*, a primrose. Duffy sat and then sank to the ground. He knew we'd be awhile. I identified the large palmate leaves of *Kirengeshoma* growing in the shade of a standard *Wisteria chinensis*, clinging to the bank above.

"I know that one," a new friend said, unlocking her knees, standing. "Doesn't it have pale yellow bells?"

Stepping past the 'Queen of Denmark' rose and her consorts, the blousy *Salvia argentea*, we paused under the peach trees. Duffy jumped, scored and lay down to munch a juicy 'Elberta', leaving us to make the journey back on our own.

Giggling about their "one of many Presidents Emeriti" and her closed door faux pas, they spotted said past president leaning over, the hem of her skirt hiked, exposing dimpled thighs. She was rooting around behind the boulder above the parking area.

Straightening, she hooted, "Look what someone just threw away." and shook the clump of Johnson grass I'd dumped there that morning. "Perfectly good, not even wilted." And with that, she dropped it into one of the plastic pots we stored behind another gate marked "Employees Only."

Thereby Entertaining Angels Unaware

There is a silence at four in the morning, like a quickening. The temperature hovering at the 32-degree mark felt cold, but somehow different. Shifting, the wind now blew across warmer waters, tracking our way, promising spring, and judging from the thundering roar, impending rain. It sounded like a flower faces in the mud kind of rain. Hair plastered across eyelashes, Wellies kind of day. A surprise of cats and dogs and wind on what should have been a party cake spring day. A washout. I rolled over, closed my eyes.

Boulders being muscled loose and shoved down the creek by a bully of white water woke me again at five, late for my scheduled marathon in the kitchen. I listened to the flood, weighing the odds. Eighty-twenty, maybe, the odds that the group of twenty-four scheduled for lunch and a talk would turn over in their Black Mountain beds and snuffle back to sleep.

My feet hit the floor. Sod's Law would have me preparing a feast, so I'd best get started. I finally found the menu I'd faxed to the Book Club president, on a drier, more optimistic day, inside a folder marked inventory. Eggplant caviar, grilled balsamic French baguettes, tomato wine soup, Quiche Sardou, fresh strawberries and kiwi and a triangle of smoked Gouda. For the sweet tray, French tart, Mousse au Chocolat a L'Orange, and freshly baked Verandah teacakes. And creme fraiche and lemon curd. I must have been feeling full of myself that day. Income to outlay? Fifty-fifty?

About then, I heard a couple of black plastic pots wash by the back door. No, we'd be eating this one, literally. Kim, stealing her own life back, was meeting with the Haywood Arts Council for breakfast to discuss their marketing needs. On my own until ten, I picked up the pace.

It's hard to remain anxious while beating eggs and whipping cream.

I started with the mousse. I'd made extra baguettes over the past few days – best for grilling with a little age on them – and that freed me to indulge in the decadence of chocolate. Breaking the bitter chocolate into squares, I placed them in a baking dish and pushed them into a low heat oven. When it reached the stage of molten cream, I stirred in the four beaten egg yolks, then the softened butter and the juice of one delectable orange. Beating the egg whites until they peaked, I folded them into the chocolate mixture. I arranged twenty-eight assorted ramekins, tiny compotes, small demitasse cups and stuck them in whatever crevices I could construct between the breakfast milk, cheese and fruits in the overstuffed refrigerator.

Pulling the latest of a long succession of tarts from the oven, I set them on the table to cool, unable to remember the whipping, the stirring.

Tomatoes from the previous September's glut thawed in the sink, and a bottle of Chenin Blanc sat on the windowsill. Later, in the shop kitchen, the tomatoes simmered, blended. Butter, salt, basil, pepper, lemon thyme, and a dollop of flour swirled through and teased to the brink of a boil; the soup simmered a little longer; then stir of soda, and cream, the soup thickened with riches. At last, I poured in the wine and heated it through.

Tomato Wine Soup

Two cups ripe tomatoes, chopped
1/4 cup butter
Two tablespoons flour
One teaspoon salt
One teaspoon lemon thyme, chopped
Two tablespoons fresh basil, chopped
Black pepper to taste
1/4 teaspoon baking soda
One cup half-and-half
1/2 cup dry white wine (Sauvignon Blanc)

Place tomatoes and butter into saucepan and simmer until soft. Allow to cool slightly and blend. Return to pan.

288

Stir in salt, pepper, basil, lemon thyme and flour. Bring to a boil. Reduce heat and simmer for five to six minutes. Stir in soda and half-and-half. Cook over low heat until slightly thickened. Do not boil. Stir in wine and heat to simmer. Cook fifteen to twenty minutes. Serves six.

I scored the eggplant for the caviar dip and shoved it in the oven, wilted the spinach, prepared the artichoke hearts and then, cheating a little, prepared the crusts for four quiches from a mix.

At 10:00 a.m., I opened the doors to rain, sweeping across the Verandah like the swales across the bow of the Pequot. And as did Ahab, I felt like shaking my fist at the elements. Instead, I slammed the door on the maelstrom and went to check the phone. No messages. If the garden club planned to cancel, they weren't sharing the information yet. Angie and Lytle, home for the summer and "so eager to work," weren't sharing either. Overdue by a couple of hours, I assumed the two jumped ship, unrepentant no-shows. The side door opened on its own floodwaters and deposited Ruby, dripping onto the mat, peeking from under the hood of her slicker.

"Shed the jacket, Ruby. It's you and me."

We dragged the tables out of the rain, dried the puddles, and began the ritual of dressing them for tea.

First, we draped old damask linens, soft as magnolia petals, over the waiting tables; then set them with Limoges, Wedgwood, Belleek, unmarked porcelain - the youngest from the '50s, the oldest from a time before the Civil War -

affordable in that they'd aged gracefully though not well. Storied teacups, saucers, bread plates, old salts, mismatched, familiar. We circled the tables, four places here, two there and on the long country table, rescued from my old barn two decades ago, six. The ritual removed me from the present into a hundred pasts. Depression glass plates giving their impression of plenty were stacked on tiers, pitted with use.

"Ruby, will you slice the kiwis?" More used to mulching and weeding in the gardens, I knew she'd hack them into chunks, at odds with the strawberries in their perfection straight from nature. Nevertheless, I thanked God for her, my true and faithful Ruby.

The quiche went in the oven.

The rain continued as we filled mesh tea balls with English Afternoon and Darjeeling. As we smeared olive oil over sliced baguettes, the rain continued to fall, bulleting off the roof, spattering the stone steps. Soaked to our ankles, we arranged fruit on grape leaves and pastries on fig and a centerpiece of old roses misted by the heavens.

As I pulled the first quiche from the oven, the telephone rang. "I'm sorry. Everyone's afraid to travel over the mountain."

And with that, the rain ceased, and the sun, piercing the scudding clouds, showered our valley with the grace of light and beauty, and us, with our pastry and tea and the absence of our partakers. Ruby returned to her gardens.

Kim stood outside in the old stone ruin of a springhouse, dubbed "The Creamery," scrubbing the mud off her shoes.

"Well, I guess I'm not late."

We sat down at a table on the silent Verandah to bask in the mountain air. Ruby crossed the parking lot, back from the gardens and stepped up to join us. Slipping off my clogs, I leaned back, closing my eyes to better hear the sound of the last raindrops dripping from the roof onto the stones. A wood thrush called memories from the hemlocks across the creek. The swooshing of tires on wet pavement...I froze, refused to open my eyes, intent on denial.

"Mom," Kim said, as if trying to soothe a high-strung horse. "It's only a Volkswagen. One."

From the sound echoing off the mountain every ten yards or so, its rotors needed turning. But at the car's top speed, if the brakes went out, it could coast to a stand-still right in front of us. Instead, it managed a four-point turn into the empty parking lot.

Long minutes passed as we watched the Volkswagen, overhanging branches baptizing it as a little zephyr twirled through the trees. A door opened. A leg swung out, then another. She must have been all of five feet tall, before time and use had bowed her back, her shoulders. Looking like she'd need ballast in a gentle breeze, she held on to the car until she regained her balance. Hovering next to the driver's side door, a younger woman in her forties, maybe fifties, peered across the roof of the car then hurried around to slip an arm under the older woman's, resting hand upon hand, guiding her, supporting her as they made their way to the Verandah.

291

So much of their story lay unmasked, there in their new floral dresses, their scuffed white sandals, their tentative smiles as they glanced at us, then dropped their eyes. They could have been my Aunt Mary and my cousin, Jill, freed at last from lives of drudgery and fear by death and divorce, still unable to untangle the web of never being quite good enough.

"We've come for tea. It's my Linda's birthday." And she patted her daughter's hand, every wrinkle in her face a beaming testament to her devotion.

"Wonderful," I said, and then she laughed, covering her mouth with a hand freckled by age and hard times. Linda just smiled and patted her mother's shoulder in return.

We sat them at the round table overlooking the creek, its rages calmed now in the sunlight, warmth soothing the troubled waters.

A remnant of amethyst silk – woven on a drawloom a century in the past, worn thin where once it spread across a prie-dieu, perhaps – covered the table. Kim served them Jasmine tea in porcelain cups. Ruby – returning from her garden and donning a leaf green apron – followed, carrying a tier of kiwi and strawberries, Brie and Edam and eggplant caviar, tomato wine soup and quiche, bruschetta with figs and feta, and teacakes and a rustic plum tart.

Their party lasted all afternoon, tea and comestibles flowing from our tiny kitchen. After all, we had plenty. Mrs. Justice (my mother would have scolded me down a notch if I'd taken liberties, called her by her given name) came from these mountains, over across the ridge in Little Laurel. Marrying at sixteen, her first baby died stillborn, followed by two boys and another little one that "died of the pleurisy."

"I waited a long time for Linda," she said.

I asked about Mr. Justice. "He died," she said. "Might I have a little more of that tea?"

Shadows stretching long, fingering the fields, cool washes of air rising off the creek, our guests rose. "I've had such a good time," Linda said.

"Thank you for my girl's happy birthday. She deserved a good one."

Glaring at me, daring me to object, Ruby shoved a potted 'New Dawn' rose toward Linda as they stood to leave. Kim deposited a sweetgrass basket filled with lavender and rose soap on the table, tucked in an envelope of Jasmine tea. I handed Mrs. Justice a bag, inside a candle shaped like a rose smelling of honey, a jar of lemon curd, what remained of the tart, and a book – *Penhaligon's Pot-Pourri of Verse and Prose, A Summer's Cup and Gardener's Nosegay.* "For Linda." We said.

Financially, the day proved to be the washout expected. But sometimes, true worth cannot be measured in coin. My take for the day? $10.00 for two cream teas, including tax. The value to the three of us – Ruby and Kim and me? Incalculable.

A Little Lagniappe for all the Angels Among Us

Vegetable Tart

    Four fresh eggs, beaten
    1/2 cup half-and-half
    1/2 cup ricotta cheese
    One cup shredded Gruyere
    One package dry vegetable soup mix
    One tablespoon chopped parsley
    One tablespoon chopped basil
    One cup butter sautéed fresh spinach, drained
    One unbaked deep-dish 9-inch pie shell
    One medium tomato, thinly sliced
    Parmesan cheese (optional)

Preheat oven to 425 degrees.

In a medium bowl stir together first eight ingredients. Pour into pie shell. Top with tomato slices.

Bake at 425 degrees for fifteen minutes. Reduce temperature to 350 degrees and bake an additional thirty to thirty-five minutes. Serves eight.

Hearts Afire

My seasonal employees arrived in one of two ways: someone in the community needed a job this side of the mountain, or they came for a visit and wanted to stay. Aiden arrived with Sarah, her partner and nemesis. While Aiden walked around enraptured, gathering four-inch herb babies into her arms, Sarah slumped along behind, arms folded, mentally tapping a foot. I saw her spark only once when Aiden walked up to me and said, "I'd love to work here."

Finding her niche, though, proved problematic. I set her up, first, in the potting shed to repot seedling basils. Arming her with an old bread knife, I showed her how to lift the fragile tots from their flat of vermiculite-topped potting soil and place them into prepared 3-inch pots, sifting fine soil mix over the roots. I came back later to find trays of basil neck-deep in soil, tiny leaves strangling from a mound of dirt, looking for all the world like a newly formed fire-ant hill.

Next, I put her to weeding. She stripped a bed of emerging yarrow, certain it was a field of noxious weeds, before I moved her to serving tea. After each encounter with a talkative table, she scurried back to the kitchen. With each new arrival to the Verandah, she hyperventilated at the thought of having to greet and pour.

Apprentice mulcher, tentative pruner, sweeper, Aiden found her place, at last, elbow-deep in dishwater, contentment emanating from her whole being as she caressed the lines of a flower-sprigged porcelain teapot. Even scouring a crusted quiche pan evoked a look of concentration and purpose. The only flies in her soapsuds the ones supplied by her partner, Sarah.

One morning I found her crying, tears splashing onto a bread pan.

"Aiden?" She turned to me and, bending from her five-foot-eight height, buried her head in my shoulder. And sobbed out her story.

Sarah, a U.S. forest ranger, was leaving to fight the wildfires in Wyoming.

"Don't worry. She'll be all right." I patted her back, striking up a there, there tempo.

At that, she wailed, "But she can't wait to leave. When I told her so, she said, 'Damn straight.' "

We spent a tearful three weeks in the kitchen before Sarah returned, smoky but resigned. Elated, Aiden began to make plans for their move to some acreage she owned abutting the national forest to live in a Yurt.

To celebrate the reunion and the Yurt, I moved her to prep – kiwis and strawberries. The kiwis survived the knife, albeit a little ragged around the edges, but we covered by adorning them with the strawberries – left whole – and topping the pair with sprigs of lavender.

I left her at the cutting board with a cantaloupe, its stem end smelling ambrosial, needing only a few Johnny-Jump-Up blossoms and a fan of tarragon leaves to decorate its slices. I headed for the garden.

Back in the kitchen, I laid the garnishes on the table and looked over at the emerging carcass of my lovely melon. I'd forgotten that not everyone grew up with a family of melon slicers and eaters. With the cleaver, she had hacked the cantaloupe in two, laid the halves face down on the cutting board and proceeded to try and saw the rind from the melon with the cleaver, ending up with a mélange of shapes – cubes, sausages, half moons, circles – all swimming in a slightly jaundiced looking soup. Tossing the potage into the blender with a little Prosecco and a bit of cream, I poured the results into crystal goblets, set adrift the violas and tarragon and called the result melon soup.

Aiden washed her way through three seasons at The Herb of Grace until winter arrived on the mountain. She came back her last spring, no longer the gangly puppy eager to please. Sarah, lasting only three days in the yurt, had moved back to Asheville for hot running water and the night life. Aiden's heart and a lot of her spirit seemed broken.

One day in early June, she failed to show. I heard she and Sarah had acquired a federally subsidized apartment in Asheville. According to my source, Sarah still felt the call of the wildfires out West and Aiden still pined for her yurt in the woods. At The Herb of Grace, we missed her.

Ladies, it's Cold Outside

We tried to warn them. The day they made the reservation. The winter, more North Dakota than North Carolina, had been glacial; and we'd opened the past Saturday as advertised, to a 28-degree morning. By noon, the temperature had soared, quivering just above freezing. Our lone customer – still coated and booted – confined her shopping to within a five-foot radius of the gas heater, asking for a warm-up of her complimentary tea every few minutes. At ten after two, with the thermometer still sulking at 33 degrees outside, the phone rang.

"The Herb of Grace," Kim answered, chipper in a frozen lips kind of way, while I poured more Darjeeling to a goose-bumped assemblage of two.

"Yes, ma'am, but the Verandah isn't enclosed and the heaters don't compete well with freezing temperatures."

Kim closed her eyes, heaved a sigh, her breath frosting the receiver. "Not for parties of eight. Maybe for two, but there's just not room..." She handed me the phone.

I heard, "...tables at one." And could only guess at the first part of the sentence.

"Excuse me. This is Bobbie. May I help you?"

What followed was a monologue devoid of pauses; wherein, I was instructed to have ready a table for eight for French Tea at one o'clock the day after tomorrow.

I sighed, much like Kim, breathing a crystalline vapor. "But, ma'am, the weather report is calling for snow..."

The call ended with, "I'll take my chances." My "no" dying somewhere in the ether of sighs.

I woke to the first pre-dawn chirp of a cardinal. Looking at the clock – six a.m. I glanced over at the thermometer. Thirty degrees and the little black arrow hovered, indecisive about its direction. Slipping on flip-flops and throwing a robe over my shoulders, I walked to the front door. Outside, the last light of a gibbous moon suffused with the first glow of a rising sun, and I could see retreating stars. Well, what do you know.

By noon, the temperature had risen eight degrees, the little arrows side-by-side companions. Kim stopped in to help, and we set the table in a small pool of sunlight at the edge of the Verandah. A fraction before one, they arrived, six of them. Removing two place settings, we slid the extra chairs against the wall.

Kim was pouring their first round of tea – Apricot and Earl Grey – when the hostess asked that we move the table, "Over there in that little alcove where the doors are. Out of the wind."

Not a lot of people arrived on our doorstep so early in the season, on a Thursday, with the weather playing coquette, and we did have the side door entrance, so Kim said, "Of course,

300

give us a moment." Calling me from the kitchen, "Oh, Mom," where I was toasting their bruschetta. I turned off the oven, grabbed a sweater, opened the door and stepped out to lend a hand.

We goose-stepped sideways, hefting and dragging the table about ten feet toward the alcove. The dusky, out of the sunlight, alcove. Then we set their chairs in place. Still clutching their coats around them, they sat, wiggled their chairs into place, glanced around, performed a little shiver. The group's hostess hailed us as we turned back to our tasks, "Wait! We'll just go back over there. Where we were." Repeating our goose steps, Kim and I settled the table in the diminishing pool of sunlight. I ducked back to the kitchen, flipped the toaster oven back on and began smearing aioli over the bread.

"Mom." I turned off the oven. Looking grim, Kim stood in the doorway. The party now wanted the table moved to the side onto the gravel, where "there's a little sun," she mimicked. This operation took a little longer. Divesting the table of its plates, cups, pots, silverware, centerpiece, we rocked, papered and scissored for who would walk backwards. I rocked to Kim's paper, but she took pity on Mama and grabbed the front end of the table.

Once on the gravel, Kim started to reset mixed patterns of vintage Haviland and Limoges while I maneuvered a six-foot patio heater off the porch, lit it and trotted back to the kitchen. A few minutes later, carrying savory sundried tomato and feta bruschetta, I crossed the Verandah, rounded the corner to hear, "Oh, the sun's gone, maybe..."

I arrived in time to see Kim lean over, her fists resting either side of a beautiful display of Lenten Roses, and in a voice deadly calm, say, "No."

As the sun moved on, the diners meekly accepted their plates of Rustic Apple Tart and humbly asked for refills of Apricot tea. At the end of the meal, they were effusive, "The bruschetta was divine, the soup heavenly." And "Lovely setting, charming accoutrements." And "Our compliments to the server."

As they started to pull out of the parking lot with smiles and waves of goodbye, Kim and I began to clear. Propped against a small silvered candelabra, an envelope bore Kim's name. Inside, one of our cards held a check with enough numbers to compensate for the trouble – almost.

Happy Birthday to Me

The kitchen was a boisterous place the morning of my birthday, and, lest I forget the milestone, members of my family had traveled north to remind me. Sandwiched between their grandparents, my sister's two little girls, Maisie and Molly, were passing Froot Loops between them, decorating their eggs and bacon. From across the table, Kim doled out advice on color and flavor choices. Waddling from the refrigerator with a glass of chocolate milk, my sister, Carla, eased into a chair, six weeks shy of deliverance. I wanted to freeze that moment or bronze it like the baby's first pair of shoes. I remember watching Kim from the steps of our house when she was little more than a toddler, trying to explain something to her dog, Chris. Pointing first at him and then at her swing set, she'd shake her head, scolding, "No." I never did figure out what Chris was failing to understand, but looking at my baby child, silver hair glinting in the sunlight, I knew what I wanted heaven to be. Moments like that — like this. Memories that you could take out whenever you wanted and walk around in them for a while.

Back in the here and now, the cereal-as-decoration moment passed into other moments, and I heaved myself from the table, poured another cup of coffee and began creaming butter with sugar, beating eggs, and sifting flour. Unbidden, Kim had given me an early birthday present by refusing to take reservations for any of our lunchtime French teas. But, as advertised, cream teas were available at any time. I never opened without teacakes, a tart or two, fresh strawberries or melon or grapes and cheese and warm yeasty bread. I could make them in my sleep or when gathering memories.

At 9:30, little girls leading the way, we trailed over to the shop, followed by one Golden Retriever, one marmalade cat, Pet, and Twig, our cat of great distinction. Twig stopped at the hill of cottage roses, sniffed one, then returned to the comforts of a warm kitchen.

After teaching the girls the fine art of gliding between tea tables and gilding them with rose petals, Kim left for a meeting, and Maisie and Molly donned their aprons. Folded over and tied, Maisie's grazed her shins; Molly's hit the top of her Barbie sandals. Requesting paper with which to write down orders, they pocketed the receipt books and pens I handed them, the weight dragging their aprons even lower.

While I opened up, Mom dusted, swept, mopped, rearranged chairs, watered plants, and, finally running out of things to do, hustled back to the garden to pick blueberries. She figured she had just enough time to start a batch of jelly.

Hiding out in the shop kitchen, Carla bellied up to the sink awaiting the first dirty dish.

I saw Ruby drive up and head toward the blueberries and my mother. I had that feeling. This was going to be a good day. August, the slowest month in our year, and the living would be easy, my family around me with time to visit. Happy birthday to me. Twenty minutes later, the first van drove up, followed five minutes later by another one, then another – a senior's group from North Georgia up for the day.

I pinged the walkie-talkies, calling Mom and Ruby to battle stations to join Carla in the prep kitchen. Maisie and Molly, order pads at the ready, stood on the Verandah. For the next hour, they glided and gilded and served bread held tight to little girl bosoms and fruit held high like crown jewels, just like Kim showed them. If I'd had time to think about it, I'd have frozen that memory as well – two tiny, dusky-haired heads, bobbing between and around, enchanting tables of graying and balding heads nodding in delight.

Still a good day.

While our Georgia visitors started their second rounds of tea, another car pulled in. Two women wearing hats and ballerina flats stepped onto the Verandah, sniffed, and called across the fully occupied tables, "Table for two for lunch."

Pulling my very pregnant sister out of the kitchen, I placed a steaming teapot in her hand, pointed, and did my best to smile. Dodging past elbows and feet, I went to greet the new arrivals.

"Hello, if you'll give us just a moment, we'll set a table for

305

you in the alcove for cream tea, if you'd like. Lunch tea is by reservation only." And I smiled my brightest.

Storm clouds gathered. Silence reigned.

"Table for two for lunch."

"I really am sorry, but lunch, French tea, is by reservation only."

"I've brought my friend to lunch."

"I am so sorry, but lunch is by reservation only. We prepare our food according to reservations."

A glare of epic proportions joined the clouds, the frost, and the silence.

I met her glare and called it with a sigh of epic proportions. I'd bent my rules so many times that John referred to them as my proposals, but there being no manna in the form of a quiche falling from the heavens, this rule remained inviolate. I tried to explain the principle of no food, no lunch. But the woman did not move, and like the Gothic villainess, her visage grew darker. Loath to blink first, I glanced away, saw two little faces, eyes huge beneath sweat-curled bangs, listening.

"Ma'am, we have never served lunch without reservations. The best I can do is cream tea. On the house." Teaching children that bullies win, I felt ashamed.

The woman whipped out one of our brochures and waved it in my face. Opening it up, she pointed with a finger manicured to the likes of Cruella DeVil. I lifted my eyebrows. Standing behind, her lunch guest cleared her throat and performed her own pointing. Printed in lovely a navy blue,

Times New Roman, bold, the words "French Tea (Lunch) by Reservation Only." marched across the page.

I seated them in the alcove. Maisie arrived soon after with a cup and saucer, face stormy. Following with a giggle, Molly held a cup dangling from her thumb and a saucer firmly held under one arm. She presented both with a smile as Maisie said, "It's my Aunt Sissy's birthday."

The afternoon sped by in a haze of humanity, humidity, and oscillating fans. The day so far? Waffling.

When the tables emptied and the vans departed, I handed each of the girls an official paycheck and their enviable tips for the day. Clutching a terracotta pot of mossy *Sagina* looking like a lawn for Hobbit gerbils, Molly asked could she have "Plantie" instead of money. Without a pause, Maisie completed the transaction, pocketing their hard-earned cash in her apron pocket as they headed down the steps, through the blue door toward home – two glossy-haired, beloved munchkins. Another golden memory for eternity.

My poor baby sister looked tuckered, legs propped on a chair, contemplating the future. Mom looked like she might be gearing up to her second wind. It's a good thing because I had one more birthday gift coming my way.

Hands on her hips, this visitor looked ready for a skirmish. Over her shoulder, I could see an upturned head of copper curls leaning out the door of a silver Saturn.

"My daughter needs a Dr. Pepper. Your road made her sick as a dog."

307

Mom rushed inside to pour a cup of tea, already half-way back before I explained we didn't have Dr. Pepper. I did have a soothing mint tea.

"What kind of place doesn't have Dr. Pepper? I've a good mind to report you."

She grabbed the cup, gulped the hot liquid, and turning, told her daughter to get herself back in the car; they were leaving.

Over at the house, John had just arrived with a bucket of the Colonel, and Kim stood over my birthday cake, knife poised. We took ourselves home.

  *   Post Script: Six weeks and one day later – his mother safely back in Florida – Caleb burst into the world, his sisters at the ready to teach him a thing or two about bullies and serving tea.

May I a Small Shop have; And many Books
(A little Adam Crowley)

Lovers of gardens tend to be lovers of books. They may grab Dirr's *How to Propagate* off the shelf, but it's Beverly Nichol's *Onward and Upward* that will win their hearts. With spade in hand, they'll drag a flat of *Penstemon* out to a patch of freshly dug earth and prop a copy of Armitage's *Garden Perennials* against a bag of compost, but when all is planted, they will see to their weariness with a dose of Mirabel Osler's *A Gentle Plea for Chaos*. And during rain showers and heat waves, or late at night when sleep eludes them, they'll turn to the classics for a spiritual history of agrarian and village life as told so well by Laurie Lee, Mary Mitford, Elizabeth Goudge.

We know we've found a new friend for The Herb of Grace when someone walks in the door and asks, "Where did you get the name for your shop?"

They looked like three generations of the same family – the same triangular faces and dark chocolate eyes, the same lively enthusiasm. But they were neighbors, having met over garden fences. Friendships formed over a love of cottage gardens.

The oldest, shoulders stooped with age or long hours with a hoe, pointed to our sign and asked about the name of the shop. I told her The Herb of Grace was an ancient pilgrim inn, the protagonist in a novel of the 1930s by British author Elizabeth Goudge. Originally built to provide sanctuary for weary travelers, in the novel, it sheltered a family, and now I wanted to be host of just such a place.

"I knew it!" Beaming, Ellen introduced herself, Ally, and Mary. She'd also introduced her friends to the novels of Elizabeth Goudge. For the next three hours, they sat at a table on the Verandah and talked books and plants and friendship. Kim arrived to pour them tea. I joined them for a minute here, a couple there, listening and thinking.

It's a memory of the senses, as fresh as a moment ago – I'm walking down the library steps, one white sandal slapping against the concrete. I don't have time to pull the strap back over my heel, I'm too busy trying to hold on to Neverland when all around me the sidewalks, the block buildings, the competing drugstores of our small town are knocking to be let back in. I'm clutching a book (greenish blue with black letters, two children, Bobbsey Twins, I think) holding it aloft, afraid I'll knock a bloom off the Azaleas planted all around me, like an ocean of white-capped waves, dappled by the sun sifting through the live oaks. Drawing the book close to my nose, I inhale and smell the fragrance of whispers of great adventures, enticing little girls into worlds without sidewalks. Then a breeze ruffles the Azaleas and the scent of stories mingles with the sweet greenness of all those blooms, forever uniting, in some kind of cosmic mystery, books and gardens and me.

An Opinionated Reader

If you've been a gardener any time at all, especially if you're a Southern gardener, you're familiar with Elizabeth Lawrence. Miss Lawrence began a garden in Charlotte, North Carolina, in 1949, and for thirty-five years, shared her experiences in her columns for the Charlotte Observer. Her book, *A Southern Garden*, is a classic and her best known work. Less well known, *Gardening for Love - The Market Bulletins*, became my favorite for the country folk peopling its pages. The book was published posthumously, edited by Allen Lacy, another Southerner who writes beautifully about gardens.

I bought Henry Mitchell's *The Essential Earthman*, seduced by the title. Described as gardener, journalist, and philosopher, Mitchell never withheld an opinion. Like, "White is commonly recommended - by the blind, I have often suspected - as a great pacifier of warring colors. I find it eggs on the warriors rather than reconciles them."

I have favorites, too, among my how-to books, referring to them again and again.

Lavender the Growers' Guide by Virginia MacNaughton
Creative Propagation, a Grower's Guide by Peter Thompson
Clematis the Genus by Christopher Grey-Wilson
And any book by Michael Dirr or Alan Armitage.

But most of all, I love those books that remind me of why I garden.

Garden Open Today, written by Beverley Nichols and set in his garden at Sudbrook Cottage in Surrey, irreverently romps you through the garden. "...critics have sometimes accused me of wandering down garden paths which never really existed, under pergolas of prose which were wreathed only in the blossoms of my fancy."

A Countrywoman's Year by Rosemary Verey

The Gardener's Year by Karel Capek

Home and Garden and *Wood and Garden* by Gertrude Jekyll

In the Eye of the Garden by Mirabel Osler

In Search of Lost Roses by Thomas Christopher

The Curious Gardener by Anna Pavord

Saving Graces by Roger B. Swain

People with Dirty Hands, The Passion for Gardening
 by Robin Chotzinoff

Home Ground by Allen Lacy

Old Herbaceous by Reginald Arkell

Beth Chatto's *Garden Notebook*

Vita Sackville-West's *Garden Book*

Chasing the Rose by Andrea Robilant

And here are a few that seem to be a blend of the practical, historical and opinionated.

The Rose Bible by Rayford Clayton Reddell

Garden Style by Penelope Hobhouse

A Garden of Herbs by Eleanour Sinclair Rohde

The Years in my Herb Garden by Helen M. Fox

Another Artiste

I held it in my hands, circled the rim with my fingertips, searching for life. It remained what it was. A container – mud brown. No – Crayola brown. None of the potter bled its way into this object. It would hold soup, but not warm it. I handed it back to the woman. "I'm sorry. I don't need any pots like this one."

In a region where wannabe potters were outnumbered only by massage therapists, more mediocrity passed through my hands than did poetry. Out of curiosity, I turned back, asked, "How much would you want for the pot?"

Turning aggressive, she said, "I'd have to have at least $50.00. It is handmade, you know."

I'd gotten better at saying no. Thank you.

Our neighbor, Millie, tells of a time when outsiders first came into this valley and discovered the beauty of handmade – brooms to sweep wide-boarded floors, walking sticks carved into a totem of crows, smoothed to reveal long days of sunshine within its heart; or willow woven into wide-bottomed baskets to hold kindling. And babies lay beneath blankets woven from the wool of family sheep, a trim of lace tickling their chins. Useful things made by hand for a spouse, a child, a neighbor, a friend should be beautiful and carry a sliver of the soul of the maker.

Well, the outsiders saw the potential, encouraged the artisans, and for a time, handmade held value.

The woman now stepping from the Verandah, pot cradled in the crook of an elbow, wanted to be a potter. She really did. She read about this area, traveled through, and caught the Appalachian fever from the mists that settle atop these mountains. And heard about the people crafting their wares along the creeks, back in the coves. Just as a child's game of gossip will end up a distortion of the truth, so did the tales of riches waiting to be paid for "art" out there in the sticks. I got a lot of these types stopping by. I saw a lot of ugly pots.

But artists, true artisans did step through our doors. On the very day of the brown bowl, just a few feet from where its maker berated my choices, a small pottery box sat upon its oaken shelf in an alcove formed by massive timbers. Smoothed and tapered, top and bottom locking together in a lovers' puzzle of indigo and lapis, the colors swirled ever higher to caress a curled leaf, a dragonfly on the wing.

The dragonfly's potter came to call one day, peeking around the twelve-foot front doors in search of the proprietor. Slipping in, she'd set a cardboard carton on the floor. It sounded heavy with its cargo of puzzle boxes. She looked up and smiled.

I'd come to know this potter, visited her in her tall house with fairy tale gables. Through a wood shadowed by majestic hemlocks and wide-spreading oaks, with birds and beasts and trolls aplenty, the path spilled us out into a sunlit glade right at the front porch. The house looked startled, as if wanting to glance quickly over its eaves, toward the barn, where the potter sat at her wheel.

In a voice soft as a southern breeze, she asked me that first day, "Do you think they will sell?"

On a small garden table sitting under the window in that same alcove, a drinking mug formed from the clay of a Cornish water meadow sat atop a small garden table. I knew without asking that the potter drank his coffee, and his tea, from just such a vessel, for there was home comfort in the fit of the mug in your hand. And there was a shallow hollow for the thumb of that hand. Freed by the potter, the figure of a small fat cow stood in bas-relief – the day's milk spilling over the figure washing it in cream. Her barnyard family – another cow, a duo of pigs, a strutting cockerel – already settling into new homes with people who loved them.

We discussed business, that potter and me, across an ocean. He at his kitchen table, me at mine. Just two country folk striking a bargain. He signed off with a "cheerio."

Still standing with her soulless bowl in one hand, the rejected potter flicked her fingers from a candlestick to a vial of lavender oil and on to a fold of old velvet. As I watched, three women crossed the Verandah and approached the doors. I always loved this moment. Struck, stilled by what they saw, they inhaled the freshet of roses and linden and fig and jasmine tea. And once again, I felt like the little girl I used to be, long past, playing at magic.

I greeted them. "Hi, ya'll." They grinned. We were back in the here and now.

The woman with the pot left as Betty Sue passed the puzzle box to her sister, Clare, and she and her sister, June, tossed for possession of the mug with the English Jersey cow.

Rhapsody in Blue

I found out early on, in drops of red-faced humiliation, that the big market vendors didn't deal with people like me. When I asked the what the minimum was for a first order, I could see their lips curl in a tight smile. "Twenty-five hundred dollars."

Some just looked over my shoulder to the next buyer, dismissing me for another customer of the right sort. It was the making of our business. Because I found other little people out there doing what they loved and wanting to share it with me. Many of them waited among the elegantly rustling pages of magazines like *Victoria* and *Gardens Illustrated*.

Under a sun recovering from overnight snow flurries, I pulled open the mailbox. Underneath invoices and advertisements, a *Gardens Illustrated* promised dreams and ideas and spring. Let the bills ferment; I needed a dose of hope. I slipped the magazine out. On the cover a picture of a frost-crusted wreath hung on a cold sky-tinted background. I shivered and it fell open in my hands, that issue of December/January, to beautiful blue shutters saturated with morning light, silvering the ochre stone of an ancient farmhouse. A field of golden flowers lapped at the foundations and the blue shutters and the blue door. I turned the page and found more blue, my favorite color, in shades and tones and tints, on linens and tables and walls. Chestnut floors, centuries-old, graced the house that could have haunted a sequel to Alice in Wonderland. I called the next morning, early.

A transplanted Brit, she was just sitting down to lunch in the kitchen of her home, the Ancienne Tannerie in the southwest of France, she said. "I'm just out of the garden. Picked this luscious tomato."

She'd worked at the vat all morning with her husband, dying sheets. Painting the fields surrounding their maison with gold, the blooms of woad stained the cloth the color of sky or sea or twilight. Yesterday, she and her neighbors, mother and daughter, sewed together peasant shirts and aprons to sell.

"Minimum? No. Whatever you like. You will be my first customer from America. I'll check the postage and call you back."

Two shirts, two chef's aprons with pocket – all a chalky blue linen – boxes of bleu pastels, and two bottles of ink the color of midnight, along with their feathered quills, flew our way two days later.

Victoria's England-inspired issue led me to Papersharks and their whimsical flour sack dishtowels – birds, pigs, cats, and chickens, as well as herbs, wildflowers, olive trees all marching in muted colors across a background of white. They remained a consistent bestseller year after year. They polished many a teapot as well.

Another small blurb about entrepreneurs put me in touch with Anna and her bracelets and earrings, sculpted roses, sweet peas, or sunflowers formed from marble dust.

Slumming it up on Palm Beach

B ut the most fun I had (And yes, it felt like playing a lot of the time.) was when I discovered the treasures hiding at country auctions, yard sales, flea markets and consignment shops.

For the first few years after we opened the shop, Kim still lived in West Palm Beach, where she owned, published, edited, and wrote most of the content for a South American trade magazine. Around midnight, she wrote press releases and designed brochures for her mama.

On an escape before the shop opened for the season, I lounged with Kim on a bench across from her apartment, looking out over the Intracoastal Waterway. A stiff breeze, heavy with the smell of *Plumeria*, plastered our hair and salted our faces. Like characters from Dickens, we sat gazing at America's symbol of opulence and wealth, Palm Beach. Just visible through the palm trees, security walls barred the way from marauding riff-raff.

Leaning back, stretching her legs, Kim told me about her run the night before my visit. Two miles along the Intracoastal, she hung a left onto Royal Park Bridge, crossed the bridge and hung another left, her feet slapping hard along the sidewalk skirting the waterway, coquina walls snubbing her as she ran. This was her regular route, following the ups and downs of the fortress walls, the subtle changes of color, the hints of wrought iron. Up ahead, the wall glowed with the color of ripe peaches in the receding light of a spent day.

It caught her eye every evening, the graceful wrought iron arches, the suggestion of being just that bit above one's neighbors. And twilight, enchanting her path, made risks seem exciting.

"Nobody was around, and it was dark enough for me to kind of blend in. I decided to scale that castle wall. See what I could see."

It went well, her True Balances gaining purchase against the roughness of the wall. One lunge and she was able to grab the top, crab-walk and then pull herself up. It went well – right up until she rose from her crouch, stood up, overbalanced and, arms swinging, fell backwards, fortunately, right into the fishy waters of the Intracoastal.

"We'll go there tomorrow."

I looked at her.

"I mean, we'll go there, to the shopping district."

And that's how we found out that the very, very rich have consignment stores too.

Kim found designer dresses, tags still on, for pennies on the dollar. I noticed a credenza near the door, where Wal-Mart stacks its impulse buy candy bars, displayed discounted items.

"Mismatched, I'm afraid. Broken sets," the proprietor said.

I picked up a small scalloped candy dish. Pale blue buds and blossoms, twined across its porcelain surface with the delicacy of a Japanese painting. Turning to the window, I peeked at the bottom. Limoges, priced at $5.00.

"As you see, there are only five bone dishes remaining in the set. If you're interested, I could cut the price to, say seventeen-dollars." Three crystal salts, one sterling-footed receiving dish, two Tiffany candlesticks, and a Chanel later, we left Deja Vu, heading back to the poor side of town.

On the Midnight Run to Morning

Shabby chic and the art of repurposing have been around far longer than the so-called lifestyle. During the dissolution of the church in England, stones from monasteries found their way into peasant pigsties. When a hole rusted in the bottom of her graniteware wash pan, my grandmother set pansies to flower in it, placing it outside the window where she'd tacked a chestnut board from the old corncrib. When I couldn't afford wooden trim for the shop corners and walls, I bought rope.

If I had a knack for taking what was to hand to supply a need, Kim turned knack into an art form, never more evident than in the days leading up to another spring. Before our doors opened for the season, she would be knee-deep in boxes obsessing over plants, teas, soaps. If the boxes had style, she flipped them over and used them as displays. Old ladders were a styling tool without equal, draped in linens, shelving toiletries, hanging pendants. Turtle shells unearthed from the creek bank made intriguing soap dishes. Old prints, yellowed with age, folded and creased, provided our menus. Opened to an interesting page, a used book with a fine cover offered up baubles to treasure seekers.

Caught mid-step between parking lot and courtyard, Kim spotted and rescued the wooden blocks, cut from the shop's pillars and beams and turned them into tables – larger ones for holding towels in the restroom, small ones finding new life as varnished cheese boards, bookends.

And according to Kim, she worked her best during the dark hours coming on midnight, the wee hours before dawn. Her preference for the creativity of the magical hours saved my metaphorical fanny on more than one season's opening.

Early spring caught me having far too much fun in the potting shed and propagation house. As if grateful for the, finally, functioning heating coils and lights, every vermiculite-topped seed tray sprouted leafy green youngsters, stocky enough for a prop house brawl to see who'd be first to the potting shed. It seemed every rose, lavender, and rosemary cutting Kim and I stuck had rooted; transforming overnight from dull and lifeless twigs to plants flushed with life. There's no mistaking that look. It pulses with energy. I'd witnessed the miracle ten thousand times, and it still transfixed me, as if Eden had thrown open its gates, inviting me in.

We were working side by side, Kim and me, soil smeared across cheekbones, foreheads, even a few flakes peppering our hair, while the Eagles "Took it to the Limit One More Time." To say we were happy would have been the grossest of understatements.

"Mom, when are you opening?"

Tipping a 'Tuscan Blue' rosemary from its pot, veins of milky white roots kicking to get out, I said, "Friday, the tenth. We gotta while yet."

"Today's Sunday, Mom. The fifth."

That's why on a mountain midnight, straddling what had been and what yet might be, a small shop was lit up like new stars, and the rafters overhead reverberated with the throaty notes of Janis Joplin belting in a new season at The Herb of Grace.

I don't know how long Kim worked – unpacking, staging. I stumbled home and fell into bed shortly before twelve. I do know she walked, or boogied, a lot of steps that night. The call I picked up the next morning before six am inferred as much. A neighbor, driving home after closing time at the Hickory Tavern, started talking before the phone reached my ear, "Well, seems there was a lot of commotion going on at that place of yours last night."

I may have hung up on him, but that would come to light another day. I had a lot to do. Easing into spring meant only a triple batch of teacakes to be made, our regular customer welcome. Our grand reopening always celebrated a week later, after we got broken in again to regular hours, no slacking off for a walk across the ridge or staying up late to read one more chapter.

After I pulled the last of the teacakes from the oven, I walked outside to watch the sun rise over the nursery beds, all the colors of God's green earth beaded with dew. A cluster of Old Spice sweet peas dropped on the way to the shop and, in the rush, forgotten, looked as if they planned to stay behind and decorate the bridge in shades of the morning sky.

I stuck my head in the barn door to say "Good Morning" to Josie and her girls. Heaped just inside, the week's emptied boxes. Shamed, I heard Kim's car headed down the road in the wee hours toward home.

"Though she be but little, she is fierce."

Crumbling, the North Wind, now but a fraction the tempest he'd once been, hung from the stone wall of the springhouse. Medusa lay face up in the chamomile lawn. Newly awakened from a thousand-year sleep, a Griffin clung to the rafters of the old creamery.

Before these creatures of myth came to stay at The Herb of Grace, their creator stepped across our garden, accompanied by unicorns, pixies and fauns, and held out a hand. My first introduction to Colleen Karcher, sculptor. She had crossed over the mountain to show us her menagerie captured in photos, then she invited us to visit her studio.

Her directions took us along a busy four-lane, winding south through the mountains, Atlanta hours in the distance. Watching for a service station, "Just before the highway exits North Carolina for the foothills of Georgia," we turned right onto gravel. A mile on, the road dwindled to a country lane hemmed in by rhododendron and mountain laurel. The path ended in an amphitheatre of hemlocks. The house, a farmer's folly from a century past, all steep pitched dormers and gingerbread, crouched center stage. Behind, a barn stepped up the hillside; from its door, we saw Colleen and her husband, David, waving us in. He looked the blacksmith he was, Paul Bunyan to his wife's Arwen Evenstar.

They took us, first, into the garden – a cloister of roses and foxgloves, bellflowers and phlox. Beasts of all ages, mystical and heraldic, hovered inside overturned pots, scaled lattice-covered pergolas. Released by the carver from their stone prisons or cast by her in tailings of gypsum and stone, they kept watch from their hidden places. We were enthralled, John and me.

Guilty of the sin of envy, I coveted them all, those children of Pan. But how could poor mortals afford such treasure? Colleen smiled and led me to a bay waiting between two mangers where she stored her weathered and broken pieces – a Griffin grounded by the loss of a wing, an East Wind mortified by the loss of his other half. I pinched enough out of the shop's meager budget that day to buy a few of both, the whole and the maimed.

But Colleen was not yet finished with us. Stepping from darkness into an incredible sky-lit space, we entered the last door. Here, slabs of marble stood about in beams of sunlight. We walked to the center of the room, directly beneath the skylight. Out of a block of marble of such pure whiteness, the eye sought relief, a wing, struggled to be free. The feathers looked silken, soft and warm beneath a human touch. I felt like weeping.

I've been privileged in this life to meet many fine artists and been subject to far too many "artistes," but as I watched

Colleen wave aside our wonder, blushing, I knew I'd never met a sweeter soul.

Lavender Blues

Outside, snowflakes the size of pansies exploded against the steps to the Verandah. Driven to a frenzy by the March wind, they sought cover against the stone walls of the creamery. The gas heater, cranked up to maximum power, managed to melt the air in a four-by-four tunnel stretching seven feet across the shop floor. The temperature gauge swaying in the draught above the counter huddled at 52 degrees. Steam percolated from the kitchen, forming droplets on the ceiling as Kim and Ruby huddled over a teakettle on the boil. Snow taunting my efforts to sweep it out the door, I just hoped I'd be able to hear a car crunching into the parking lot in time to dig a welcome to the front door. The Grand Spring Re-Opening at The Herb of Grace was underway.

With the shop closed, January and February constituted downtime, income a faintly remembered hope. But every horticultural gift and gourmet food show in the East opened those months in full seductive swing, "Buy now, pay later. Buy now, pay later." Now "later" had rattled the door and I was ripe for the ringing of the telephone. I said "yes" at the first spoken syllable of the word reservations.

"Mom." Kim stood, hands on hips, just inside the door.

"Yes?"

"We only have twenty-five chairs. We only have twenty-five plates – if we rob the shop's inventory. It looks like a Perry expedition outside and feels like one in here. So, tell me again how many you booked for French Tea on the Verandah? For the day after tomorrow."

"Fifty. It seemed like a good idea at the time."

Ah, spring in the mountains. What a tease.

The sun kissed the garden with a 62-degree sparkle. Beneath the magic tree, hellebores had shuddered free of the snow, but the 'Grosso' lavender, hedging the gravel walk, still bore its winter coat of smoked plum. On the Verandah, a seething tide of herbalists, drunk on the promises of spring, called for more bread. Ruby, having informed me her waitressing days were over, crouched over the sink elbow-deep in suds. In a finely choreographed routine, Kim and a high school neighbor were dumping saucers and cups into the sink, plucking clean plates out of Ruby's hands and toweling them dry before waving them by me. With a flourish, I placed a sliver of tart, a fan of kiwi, and a slice of Ingles cheddar – dressed up as Farmhouse, purloined from the neighbor's refrigerator – upon each and sent them out to the simmering tea takers. Waiting for spring had made hibernating herbalists ravenous.

I glanced at the clock, three hours and they'd finally stopped eating. Satiated, they listened to a talk on the herb of the year, lavender. When the speaker – a Valkyrie dressed in a delusion of fairies and Cicely Mary Barker, all rose chiffon and velveteen slippers – mentioned the soporific quality of lavender, one of the back tables huffed a snore.

Ladders tipped out of the barn, stools drug from the attic, packing boxes turned upside down and draped with muslin labored along the perimeter of the Verandah, proclaiming the beauty and uses of lavender. Smelling of honey collected in far-flung fields, a dove gray box held French soap milled with lavender. Antique silk remnants, sewn into sachets by our neighbor, Linda, were stuffed with our dried lavender and displayed in a vine basket woven by my mom and given a lavender color-wash by Kim the night before. The Verandah steps preened under a splattering of purple paint.

I'd pulled all the books with even a passing mention of lavender off the shelves and stuck them between displays and stacked them along the porch railings. Draping tea towels, screen-printed with woven wands of lavender, over the rungs of a ladder, we positioned upon its steps bottles of lavender oil and tins of lavender tea and lavender sugar.

But the true stars of this extravaganza, verdant shrublets of lavender in 4-inch pots, flaunted themselves from tables, from counters, from windowsills, even from the restroom sink:

* *Lavandula x intermedia* 'Grosso,' 'Provence,' and 'Dutch' which hold up so well in Southern humidity when planted in grit and mulched with stone.

*More lavandins – 'Grappenhall,' 'Seal,' and the silvery leafed dandy, 'Fred Boutin',

*English lavenders (*Lavandula angustifolia*) – the ubiquitous 'Hidcote' with its rich purple bloom on stubby stems and a witch's broom of a body and its paler cousin 'Munstead', soft pink 'Jean Davis' and 'Vera', which has some of the finest oil and a white flowered variety, shy to bloom, but so beautiful with silver gray leaves that look full and lush even after torrential rain.

These plants, taken from cuttings stuck at the beginning of an early winter, nursed and pinched as babies and cosseted winter-long in a poly tunnel, had sucked up the expensive formula of propane heat and sodium lighting to become plump and supple bairns. By June, they'd be in the flush of blooming youth.

The speaker wound down, eaters pushed back chairs ready to scramble, and finally take on a different role, that of shopper.

They were gone, the last herbalist retreating over the mountain. Silence descended. Feet propped up on chairs, we sipped the dregs of some tomato wine soup Kim had unearthed in the devastation of the kitchen. Ruby nudged a copy of *The Lavender Garden*, fallen from its makeshift book railing, to one side with the toe of her clog, saving it from a dollop of Boursin slowly crusting over. A smattering of 4-inch lavenders lay upended, looking like they had failed to survive their playgroup. A lone French soap, gouged and rejected, cowered in a corner of the display cabinet. Trotting a total of eleven times on the 400-yard trek – down the steps through the garden door, across the gardens, over the bridge, past the drive to the tunnels for "a 'Grosso' that matches this one" – I was snockered. Ruby's total was seven for "what else have you got?" Kim, asked for the third time if she could go get a 'Provence' a little less lopsided, took the last long suffering lavender from the man's demanding grip, pinched off a branch and handed it back to him. He said thank you.

One of our crew had grabbed an armful of dried nosegays languishing in a cupboard, slapped them in a harvest basket and sold the lot of them for $5.00 a piece. Several – stems of 'Provence' wound around single velvety blooms of the old *Rosa gallica* 'Tuscany' – still smelled of lavender and roses three summers on.

Frenzy over, fever spent, we slumped, bedraggled.

"How'd we do?" Ruby asked.

"Let's see."

I offered them French Tea at a cut rate. I gave them a ten-percent discount on plants, sold shop items discounted fifteen-percent, and offered garden books at a twenty-percent reduction. Levering myself from a pike position, I hobbled over to the counter. Opening the cash drawer, I riffled through the bills, scrambled the change, and totaled the credit card receipts. It was close, but I might just break even.

I looked out at my crew, saw their eager, puppy dog expressions; thought about the endless questions they'd answered, the grueling miles they'd navigated, their constant smiles and humor and graciousness, and I answered, "Great. Just great."

Befuzzled, Bothered and Bewildered

Furtive, like a mouse gauging its chances to make it to the hole in the wall, she scurried in, huddling just inside the door. She looked like someone on the run – if her Mary Janes had looked less orthopedic, if her beaded, velour pantsuit hadn't matched her socks and the bow in her hair and her purse and her umbrella. Maybe she'd ditched her tour bus on its way to the casino.

"Good Morning."

No reaction at all. As if we moved in separate dimensions, paralleling in a small shop in the Twilight Zone. I watched her approach a cabinet as if mesmerized. She stretched out her hand, rose to her toes. Grabbing a small mantle clock, enameled and gilded at least fifty-years ago, she cradled it in the crook of her right arm.

I tried again, "Hello."

She tipped her head – a murmur from the spirit world – and darted to a galvanized garden table, snatching up first a bundle of tapers smelling of honey and fig, then another of lavender. Clutching them to her bosom, she stole a glance my way and continued her circuit clockwise around the shop.

"Would you like me to take those?"

Startled, she whirled my way, a breakthrough.

As soon as her hands were empty, she grasped the edges of a Venetian mirror that had come to life a hundred years ago near the shores of the Adriatic Sea. When I'd first seen it, leaning against the tailgate of a Chevy Silverado between a reproduction Coca-Cola sign and a stack of *National Geographics* at a flea market outside Georgetown, South Carolina, I'd coveted it. Like Midas and his gold, like Gollum with the ring. I reached out, touched it.

"How much?" I'd asked the red-bearded vendor.

"How about forty?"

It was mine.

I'd brought it back to the shop, slapped an astronomical price on it, ensuring my possession would remain inviolate.

The woman didn't glance at the price tag. I caught the mirror as she freed it from its hooks and laid it next to the clock. She tossed a ribbon-tied pair of old damask pillowcases over the mirror.

By the time she'd circled to the door again, she had accumulated tea towels in black and white; French toiletries in Milk and Honey and Fig and Myrtle; hand molded pottery bowls, thumbed and fingered with impressions of mystical beasts; tea; jewelry; books. And she'd dragged one of our bistro chairs and a tall bay topiary off the Verandah and over to the counter. Stitch by stitch, the calculator spit tape as my fingers clicked keys. I'd be an hour, or more, putting everything back in its place. Wondering in what universe she might now dwell, and if sound might penetrate, I announced the total. She pulled out her Visa card.

At five minutes past closing time, I began shutting windows against the chill of the oncoming night. The phone rang. Bill from the Warm Springs Inn cleared his throat.

"Bobbie, I'm trying to find a missing guest. I haven't seen her since last night, but I know she's been back. There's a bunch of stuff on the bed and one of your receipts on the bathroom sink. Her family's called looking for her, said they haven't heard from her all week. Been calling every B & B in the mountains, apparently."

I checked my bank account twice a day over the next week, called Bill every day for word. I made payroll, but I waited to pay the credit card bill, mourning the loss of my mirror. Three weeks later, I got a call from Mrs. Trumpeter's daughter. Her mother was back home in Detroit, and the mirror looked lovely hanging over the television set.

Rings and Things

The sun setting on day three of the Atlanta Market found John and me gawking, searching and poking amid the Temporaries on floor three. Fatigue settled at my knees, and walking felt like exercising in mud. Longing for a place to sit in a world where sellers concentrated on keeping you moving, I spotted a slice of horizontal beam between booths and headed for it. I leaned my head back and sighed, which brought my eyes level with an old oak dresser. Bibelots, curios in shades of amber and toast and shell, draped themselves over an open drawer. Hanging from a long strand of amber-colored beads, a nest of glistening mahogany threads held an opaline button in all its iridescent beauty. I'd seen a cousin of that button while playing in my granny's closet, where she hoarded her old purses and shoes.

I stood up. The whole booth held treasures harvested from attics and memories. The vendor's name scrolled across a large beveled mirror introduced us to "Grandmother's Buttons." How appropriate. The seeds for all things vintage sprouted in places like this back in the 90s – one woman ideas, one woman shows, one man shows. Being a first-timer without a permanent home at the market, "Grandmother's Buttons" befriended the small shops like ours, enticing us with low minimums, low prices, and uniquely beautiful temptations.

A pair of these earrings – dangling, bronze-hemmed jet buttons, I think – brought Polly to us. From over the mountain, she'd seen Kim's press release when it showed up at the newspaper's editorial office. Plants and jewelry, she said she couldn't ask for more.

The next time she dropped over the mountain, Jo and Katherine from her lacemakers' group came with Polly for tea. They sat at a table overlooking the lavender garden with a view through the large café doors into the shop. The stepladder, used for displays since Kim drug it from the barn and painted it lilac, stood just beyond the library table draped in vintage linens. Katherine told me later, she picked out two crocheted dresser scarves, a cross-stitched tablecloth, and a pair of monogrammed pillowcases, all while munching lavender teacakes and sipping smoky Royal Gunpowder tea. Jo headed for the books and Polly a necklace of silver braids and pearl buttons.

And Polly wanted a garden, too. I met her husband and her son when I dropped off the Japanese maple, the 'Blue Princess' holly, the ferns and the perennials in preparation of making a garden outside her front door.

Over the years, we talked of plants and jewelry and family. When her parents visited from Georgia, she brought her mother out for tea. My mother met Holly and her cronies pinching rosemary when she and my dad came up for a week in April.

When Polly found out John was on the lookout for the perfect salsa – the kind to make you tear up without breaking into a sweat – she brought him a jar from her dad's stash. Then later gave him the recipe. Only friends do that.

Salsa Recipe

Prepare 6 jars (if needed)

    7 cups chopped tomatoes (juice drained)
    2 medium onions chopped
    1 cup vinegar
    2 jalapeno pepper chopped
    1 T salt
    2 cayenne pepper chopped
    1 T black pepper
    1 bell pepper or 2 large banana peppers

Medium heat until boiling. Simmer for an hour.

A Time to Weep

Her allotted days having been numbered and spent, Hope left us in her twenty-first year, leaving our valley bereft without her. From its sacred place atop a snow swept hill, Pleasant Grove Chapel, lights glowing, guided those who loved her and gathered us within its old walls.

We were neighbors, drawn here to mourn, to offer comfort to Callie, to Sam, if any such thing existed for this family. Losing a child is a singular grief, like no other, and it is beyond description, beyond solace. The width of the sanctuary separating us expanded to a thousand acres as I began my walk across to Callie. Everything I thought of to say seemed too small, too trite, in such vast wells of sorrow. The journey to her side stretched to days, but was over in seconds. I meant to reach out, hug her, but I felt her tremble, like a seismic shift her imperceptible retreat. Instead, she reached out, patted my hand, and turned away. For Callie, composure to get through this day seemed dependant upon constant movement, from one person to the next, forfeiting comfort, lest the hollowness

341

inside her proved fatal, and she had two other children to think of.

The memorial service began with "Amazing Grace," that most holy of redemption hymns. Tears baptized the scars of the old church piano as Callie's brother played and the gathered sang.

A CD of Hope's favorite songs provided background to a slide show of her precious days on this earth – good and bad. At the age of three or four, Hope, standing in the sand, the ocean lapping at her feet. The first day of school she stands by a mailbox, a Barbie lunch box swinging from her hand. She's waving a flag, her grin spread wide as Sam holds her aloft over the heads of the crowd, her wheelchair at his feet sitting empty. Her eighteenth birthday, her brittle spine crumbling, hunched like a character from Grimm, the grin still there.

Outside, the storm faded and sunlight sifted through the windows of the timeworn church, and Sam began to tell us the story of Hope's life, his voice raw with grief. As he stumbled to find words, his hand touched, smoothing, again and again, the breast of his white shirt where creatures, stitched in silk, paraded through a mystical forest of green thread – Hope's work, her gift.

I know there were baked meats. Country people do not grieve empty-handed. I only remember the taste of ashes.

The service over, we all slipped into our cars to head down the mountain road, turned icy in the shade of the hemlocks standing like sentinels, leaving Callie and Sam, their two little boys, and a sorrowing grandmother alone in the little church.

With such cruelty does the sun rise on grief. Life goes on, as they say. For me, one week, two passed in hours and days laboring in the hoop houses, while winter laid siege a final time. I heard the phone ringing as I sloshed through melting snow toward the house, the back door ten feet away. As I picked up speed, I heard the sucking sound of determined mud. Grabbing the receiver, I said, "Hello," and watched my right Wellie filling with snow.

On the other end of the phone, Callie asked a favor. I said, "Yes." And waited for her request. Would I open the shop for her for just a few minutes? There was something there she needed.

With the vendor, I'd agonized over the price, but in the end ordered two. Etched sterling silver hands grasping a small vial of faceted crystal, designed to hold floral water or holy water, perhaps, hung suspended from a fine silver chain. In the alcove tucked between two tall poplar columns, the amulets waited while all around them more mundane artifacts – onyx necklaces, dangling amber earrings, Victorian brooches – were sold, to be replaced by others that sold again. At last, the first amulet left with a hurried shopper in the final week of our holiday clearance. The other remained, draped across a small iron mirror.

Now, Callie reached for the crystal amulet, held it for a moment, tilted it toward the tall windows, watching it fracture the eternal light into pieces of gold. Then she rested it against her heart.

"Hope's ashes. To hold just a bit of her, here with me."

343

Forgotten and Lost

On the afternoon Millie found her mother hanging from the porch rafters, she'd been married only a few months, still a year away from the birth of her only child. And even then, their future was being decided half a world away – an apocalypse to make the tragedy of her mother little more than a sentence in the conversation of our friendship.

As near as I can remember, she told me of her mother's suicide over our first glass of ice tea together. The brutal and lonely beauty of the hollows, the gorges rippling this ten-mile strip of Appalachia could haunt a man and twist a woman's mind.

"She'd been acting kinda strange for a while."

Another day early on among the dregs of a shared pot of coffee and blueberry muffins, Millie sorted through more of her memories of the home and the farm – down the road a piece, across a creek and a hundred yards up a sassafras cove – where she and her husband, Cecil, raised tobacco and chickens and sold eggs.

"My boy, Aaron, was an only child. There were a lot of onlies in this valley. They'd claim now it was something in the water. Might of been. Anyway, there was this hundred-foot poplar..."

And she's back under that tree, sunlight slicing through its forks illuminating a tumble of lichened boards across the creek, looking up at her little boy pitching rocks down into the water, splashing two old roosters.

"Most days, Cecil'd sleep till noon, so Aaron helped collect and clean the eggs. The truck'd come over the mountain twice a week. Take the eggs to Asheville. Then it stopped coming. I drove a school bus after that. Twenty years."

The mountain roads she spoke of twisted and turned a total of thirty-nine times to cover a distance of a few miles before it emptied onto a state highway. The loop into Millie's chicken farm would have made it an even forty. The bus route took in those forty, added another fifteen miles of river curves and ended at the rock school, circa 1919, in the 'flats'.

"Aaron's class was the last to graduate from the school. Consolidation come along and took our younguns out of the valley and the heart out of the community. Aaron graduated college from over to Mars Hill. Was going to be a geologist. Instead, he joined the Marines. Shipped out to Vietnam. Helicopter pilot. First Lieutenant."

Millie lifted her hand, shook a bracelet encircling a wrist swollen and knotted with arthritis. On June 3, 1967, during an extraction mission in Laos, Aaron's helicopter and all crew aboard went down. Etched into the copper band and into Millie's heart were the letters MIA.

345

During those first weeks on the creek, Millie often stopped by to offer details of her life, lifted like pebbles from the wellspring of her history. After those early days, she seldom mentioned her losses, only a memory now and then, fleeting in its delivery. Instead, she traded in gossip. Hunker down though we might, hoping to stay out of her crosshairs, none of us here escaped her seasoned critiques.

Like a specter, she haunted those of us new to the creek, popping up when least convenient, materializing inside closed doors. Claiming all who stumbled into her ancestral territory as a project in need of a fix, she clucked after us like a mother hen, and the burden weighed heavy, as did the guilt for our uncharitable thoughts. I thought it was only me that found her so wearying until I saw the relief on Callie's face when a newly arrived couple broke ground for a home, one curve up the hill from Millie's, releasing Callie from an unrealized burden.

After the last brick settled into its mortar, the transplants, two young women, followed a moving van with Atlanta plates and drove up to their new door, leaded glass lights sparkling under the noon-day sun.

Hearing Millie's, "They must have money to burn," down at the cafe, we all felt grateful to the new blood for the coming reprieve and just a little ashamed of ourselves.

Not long after, Millie, seeing me at the mailbox, stopped to tell me of the amusements of the day before. "Soaked in the hot tub down at the Springs right up to dinner time."

It seemed the three – Millie and Pat and Deb – got on like a house afire, and I grew used to seeing her ride by with a wave from the passenger seat of Pat's Land Rover. Days passed without a homily or a well-aimed barb, weeks without Millie's head popping up at the window, nose flattened to the glass.

If I'm truthful, I lost track of time, and of her, and of how long it had been since I'd seen her or made any kind of effort to. But retribution lay ahead for the sin of procrastination and neglect. Shame and coals heaped upon my ungrateful head.

Millie's brother at my door in his overalls, boots caked with a day's work, telling me he thought we'd want to know. Five days in the hospital and, "I'll be taking her ashes over to our old home place."

How we failed to feel the thunder at her passing, I'll never know. But I will forever regret the selfish busy-ness that kept me from a last goodbye.

As the snow melted from the ridge tops and spring began to flush the coves and hollows with its hundred shades of green, we resumed our lives along the creek.

Then twenty-one times the sun rose and set, bringing us to a day quite ordinary in all respects, save the one. The news reached us from across the mountain. And left us wondering if the likes of Punchinello, the clown macabre, had been chosen to orchestrate such fate in such a manner.

In the jungles of Laos, where hell could devour its kill before the smell of napalm evaporated from its skies, fragments of bone were unearthed, identities verified, and a lost son found his way home. And in the face of such terrible irony, we wondered anew if the bell tolled with cosmic cruelty or rang with divine mercy. But by then, Millie had traveled beyond reach of the one, to bask in the love of the other, as mother and child – two parts of the same soul – were reunited in that incomprehensible Somewhere. A tall tree, a rippling creek, a splash, and the sound of laughter.

And This Too Shall Pass, My Child

We're sitting on the Verandah, performing what has become a ritual here. Kim is pouring the last of the tea, Ruby slicing the leftover heel of a baguette, Maree collecting cheese and fruit and a little Boursin - extra from today's Cream and French teas - and assembling it on a paper towel as if the paper is the finest of porcelains. I'm passing around a menagerie of cups and plates. We're breaking bread together at the end of the day. The last of the lingering customers drove away a few minutes ago. The closed sign swings from the chain pulled across the entrance.

We finish. Maree and Ruby leave together, headed toward their cars parked next to the greenhouses. Kim and I sit on the steps leading down to the road and the creek. Most of the commuters have passed by, making their way home. All is quiet, except for the sawing of the cicadas, and the splash of a frog taking a late swim, and, as ever, the eternal sound of rushing water.

It has been a good day. Busy. But not too busy. Four sorority sisters, lunching throughout forty years of living, enjoyed French Tea, marking yet another memory. The three

Wiccas, passing their monthly sojourn on the Verandah, slurped several pots of complimentary tea, whispering incantations of friendship. From over the mountain, our chamber friends ordered cream tea, and then asked, chagrined, if we had enough quiche and soup to upgrade to the full French Tea. We did. Pete and Wayne dropped by, stayed for tea, and left with roses, 'Mme Isaac Perrier' and 'Marie Pavie', lovely ladies to accompany them to their garden in the downhill dales of Tryon.

"Gotta go, Mom." Kim leans in to hug me. I hug her back, holding on.

"Thanks for coming to help," I say.

"Sure."

We say "I love you" together on the same exhale.

I'm alone now, on the steps, witness to the gloaming settling over the mountains, the mists rising from the waters across the way. With the fading away of the day, the dark will come. There are no dusk to dawn lights on the creek, and the closest neighbors, supper lights burning, hide beyond the twisting road. My foot brushes the lavender that swoons onto the steps. A smell so familiar, so beautiful, it makes my heart ache. The breeze swirls off the face of the mountain and carries with it a smell of leaves and damp and moss, so fecund it needs only the breath of God to spring to life.

I hear the swoop of batwings close and catch sight of a quartet, barely visible, darting black against deepening indigo sky. Perhaps they're from the colony that sleeps among the rafters of our barn - oblivious company to our daily comings and goings. A rustle in the brush, a taint of wildness on the breeze, lets me know a raccoon watches from the creek. The last call from a wood thrush, sounding of sorrow, floats from the ridge above the house.

Night is here now, the moon not yet risen, but the stars pierce the eye, brilliant in their numbers, humbling in their glory. I grab the flashlight I brought from behind the counter and rise. I will make my way home. Disturbing a frightened explosion of doves in my gracelessness, I point the flash at my feet and walk on. Beyond the small cone of light, all manner of creatures susurrate, pip, slither. So I am not alone after all.

Stumbling between the buttresses of smokehouse, of springhouse, I catch a whiff of mint. Down the steps, through the blue door. Crushed fruit smell. I must be near the blueberry bushes. The rhubarb-nested stone jar is close. I swerve to avoid trampling the leaves and am caught, enveloped in the fragrance of night blooms – *Nicotiana, Datura,* Moonflower.

Ahead, the house is dark. I forgot to leave a light burning, and John's a state away. Flashlight still aimed at my feet, I bump against the fence, grope for the handle, feel the roughness of wood, and swing it open. I catch Duffy sleeping, and he scrambles to his feet, shamefaced. A few steps and I'm at the door. My hand finds the switch. Let there be light. It's been a good day, and I'm home. Until tomorrow.

Then what once was, became what would no longer be. A hope no longer real. A dream no longer true.

Up ahead, the trees scatter to reveal a small house, enchanted, rendered from solid earth, roof impossibly steep, clinging to tumbled stone banks. And if you listen, really listen, even now you will hear the clink of a teapot against a cup and the murmur of voices across a wide verandah and feel the magic floating in on the breeze. Like a dream, The Herb of Grace - nursery, shop, gardens and tearoom - forever echoing laughter and memories. I like to think of it there, still.

Bobbie and John and *Kim*

"Weeping may endure for a night, but joy cometh in the morning."

Psalm 30

Made in the USA
Columbia, SC
22 December 2021

51025519R00214